ALFRED'S BASIC ADULT
THEORY PIANO BOOK
LEVEL ONE

WILLARD A. PALMER   MORTON MANUS   AMANDA VICK LETHCO

INSTRUCTIONS for USE

1. This book may be assigned at the FIRST LESSON, when the student reaches page 7 of Lesson Book 1 of Alfred's Basic Adult Piano Course. Assignments should be made according to the instructions in the upper right hand corner of each page of the THEORY BOOK, which is co-ordinated with the LESSON BOOK page by page.

2. Every concept and principle introduced in the Lesson Book is reinforced in this book. Additional drills in note recognition make it a valuable aid in developing reading skills. Important tips are presented that make learning chord progressions easier. Reviews are presented in the form of games and puzzles.

3. Theory lessons should be completed by the student AT HOME, and checked by the teacher at the next lesson.

2

Assign with page 7.

Name That Key!

To learn the names of the piano keys fluently, it is very beneficial to practice naming them in a random order, rather than counting up the keyboard alphabetically. When each key can be quickly recognized by its position in or next to a 2 or 3 black-key group, you will always know exactly which key you are playing.

C is on the **LEFT** of any 2 black-key group!

1. Find all the C's on this keyboard. Print a C on each one.

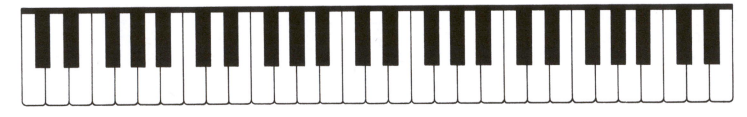

E is on the **RIGHT** of any 2 black-key group!

2. Find all the E's on this keyboard. Print an E on each one.

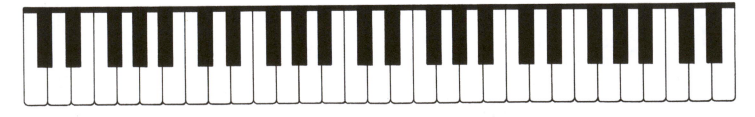

D is in the **MIDDLE** of any 2 black-key group!

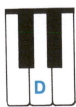

3. Find all the D's on this keyboard. Print a D on each one.

Assign with page 7.

F is on the **LEFT**
of any
3 black-key group!

4.   Find all the F's on this keyboard. Print an F on each one.

B is on the **RIGHT**
of any
3 black-key group!

5.   Find all the B's on this keyboard. Print a B on each one.

G is **BETWEEN** the
1st & 2nd keys
of any
3 black-key group!

6.   Find all the G's on this keyboard. Print a G on each one.

A is **BETWEEN** the
2nd & 3rd keys
of any
3 black-key group!

7.   Find all the A's on this keyboard. Print an A on each one.

The Treble Clef Sign

Assign with page 8.

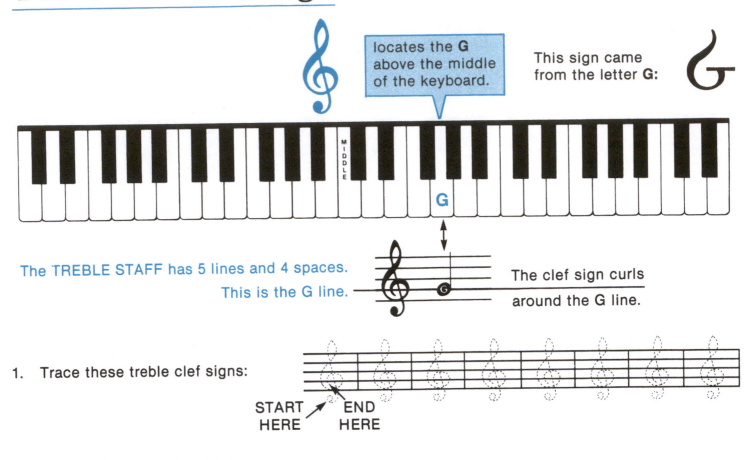

locates the **G** above the middle of the keyboard.

This sign came from the letter **G**:

The TREBLE STAFF has 5 lines and 4 spaces.

This is the G line.

The clef sign curls around the G line.

1. Trace these treble clef signs:

START HERE → END HERE

2. Draw a line of treble clef signs.

The notes of the RIGHT HAND **C POSITION** are written on the TREBLE STAFF.

Middle C is written on a short line below the staff, called a *leger* line. D is written in the space below the staff. Each next higher note is written on the next higher line or space.

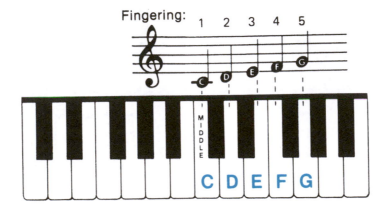

3. Write the name of each note in the box below it.

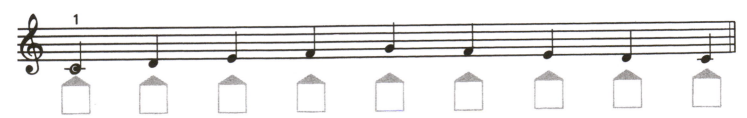

4. These notes are on **LINES.** Write the name of each note in the box below it.

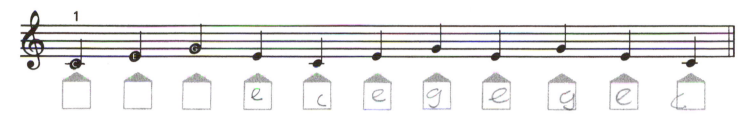

5. These notes are in **SPACES.** Write the name of each note in the box below.

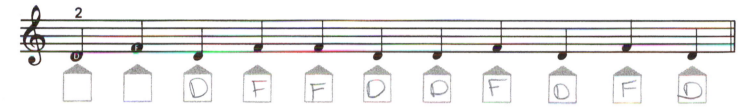

6. Here are notes on **LINES & SPACES.** Write the name of each note in the box.

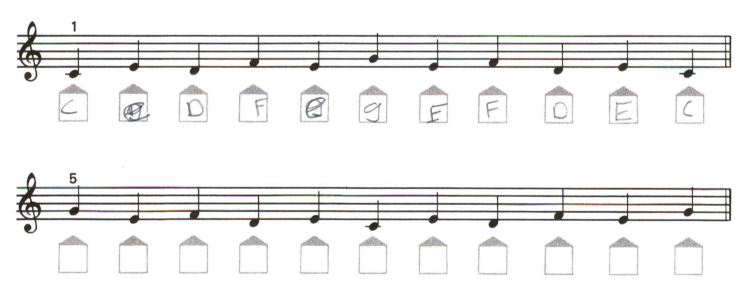

7. When a note repeats on the **SAME** line or space, the note is repeated on the keyboard. Write the name of each note in the box below it.

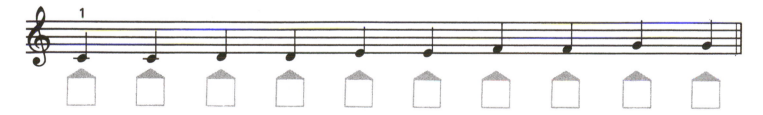

8. Above each note on this page, write the finger number used to play it in RH C POSITION.

9. Play all the notes on this page in RH C POSITION.

The Bass Clef Sign

Assign with page 10.

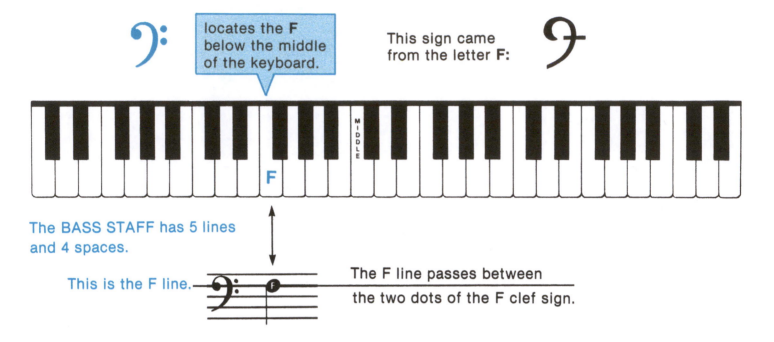

locates the **F** below the middle of the keyboard.

This sign came from the letter **F:**

The BASS STAFF has 5 lines and 4 spaces.

This is the F line. — The F line passes between the two dots of the F clef sign.

1. Trace these bass clef signs:
   Always begin on the **F** line.
   The 2 dots are in the TOP 2 SPACES.

Start here.　Make the 2 dots last.

2. Draw a line of bass clef signs.

The notes of the LEFT HAND **C POSITION** are written on the **BASS STAFF.**

The C, played by 5, is written on the 2nd space of the staff.
Each next higher note is written on the next higher line or space.

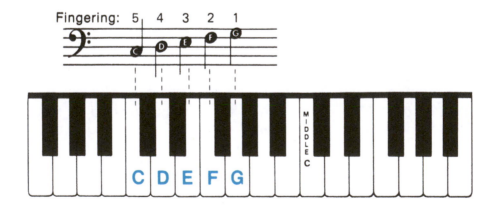

Fingering: 5 4 3 2 1

C D E F G

3. Write the name of each note in the box below it.

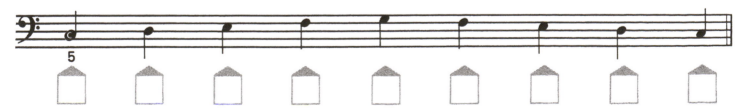

5

Assign with page 10.

4. These notes are in **SPACES.** Write the name of each note in the box below it.

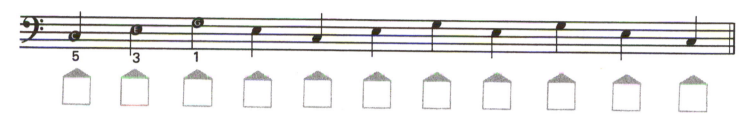

5. These notes are on **LINES.** Write the name of each note in the box below.

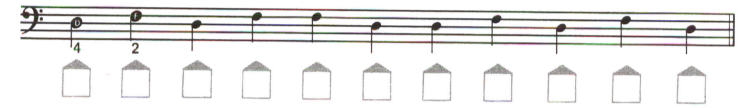

6. Here are notes on **LINES & SPACES.** Write the name of each note in the box.

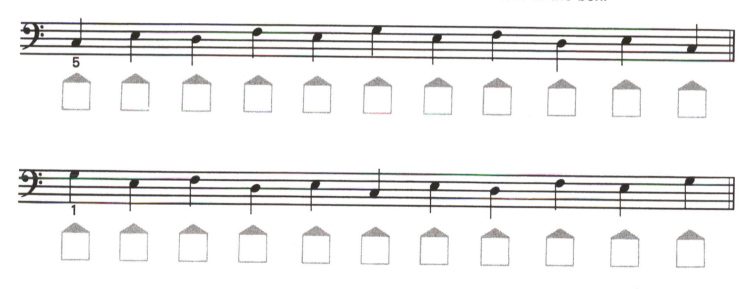

7. Each of these notes repeats on the **SAME** line or space. Write the name of each note in the box below it.

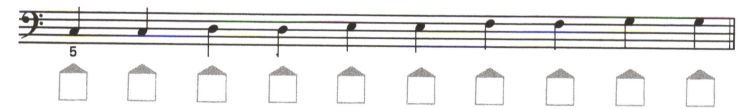

8. Below each note on this page, write the finger number used to play it in LH C POSITION.

9. Play all the notes on this page in LH C POSITION.

8

Assign with page 12.

The Grand Staff

Piano music is written on a GRAND STAFF derived from a staff of 11 lines.
The notes are named for the first 7 letters in the alphabet, repeated over and over:

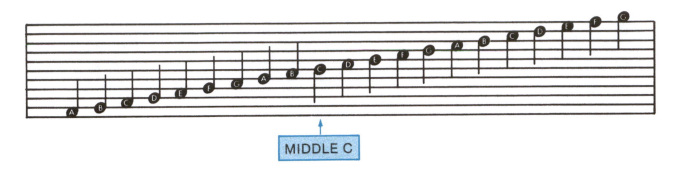

MIDDLE C

Since reading from so many lines would be difficult,
CLEF signs were devised to mark the F, C, and G lines:

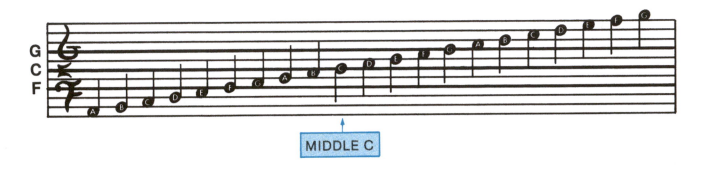

MIDDLE C

In modern music, the GRAND STAFF is separated into 2 smaller 5 line staffs (joined by a brace) for easy reading.

The middle line is omitted. Instead, MIDDLE C is written on a short line, called a LEGER line, which is added only when needed.

The F CLEF SIGN became our modern BASS CLEF SIGN 𝄢,
which still locates F below middle C.

The G CLEF SIGN became our modern TREBLE CLEF SIGN 𝄞,
which still locates G above middle C.

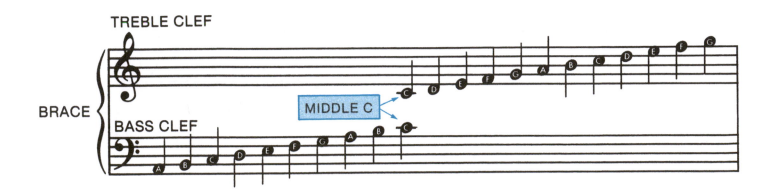

This explains why the names of the lines and spaces of the BASS STAFF are different from those of the TREBLE STAFF. For ease in reading, it is still best to think of the GRAND STAFF as being ONE CONTINUOUS STAFF.

Assign with page 12.

1. Print the letter names on this keyboard, beginning with the lowest A and ending with the highest G. You should use the complete MUSICAL ALPHABET 3 times.

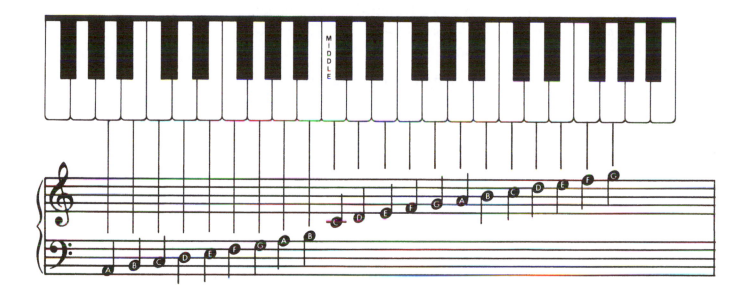

2. On the GRAND STAFF above, draw a circle around the 5 notes you have already learned in the BASS CLEF and the 5 notes you have learned in the TREBLE CLEF.

3. Write the name of each of the following notes in the boxes.

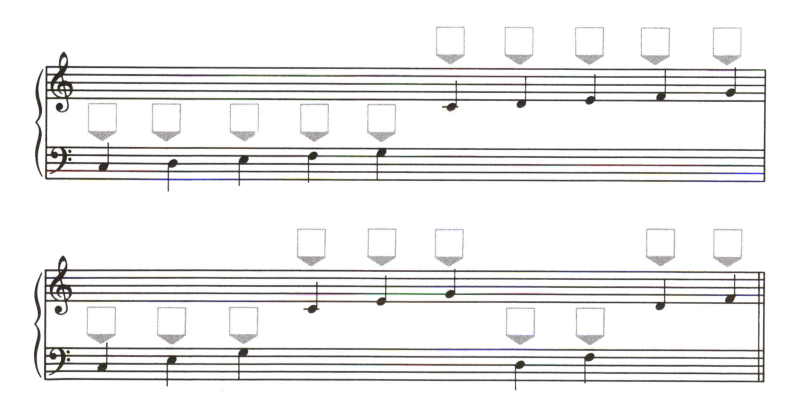

4. Write the finger numbers used to play the above notes in C POSITION. Write the numbers for TREBLE notes ABOVE the notes. Write the numbers for BASS notes BELOW the notes.

5. Play the notes.

10

Assign with pages 12-13.

The Time Signature

Music has numbers at the beginning called the **TIME SIGNATURE**.
The **TOP NUMBER** tells the number of beats (counts) in each measure.
The **BOTTOM NUMBER** tells the kind of note that gets ONE beat (count).

$\frac{4}{4}$ = 4 beats to each measure.

     = **QUARTER NOTE** ♩ gets ONE beat.

	NOTE	COUNT	TOTAL NUMBER OF COUNTS
QUARTER	♩	"1"	1
HALF	♩	"1 - 2"	2
WHOLE	𝅝	"1 - 2 - 3 - 4"	4

1. In the box under each note, write the number of counts the note receives.

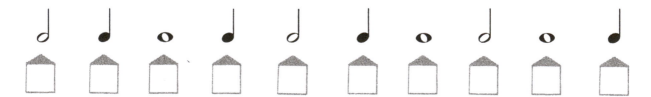

BAR LINES divide the music into MEASURES. Each measure in $\frac{4}{4}$ time has notes adding up to 4 counts.

2. Complete each measure by adding just one **G** to each, so the counts add up to 4:

3. Complete each measure by adding just one **C** to each, so the counts add up to 4:

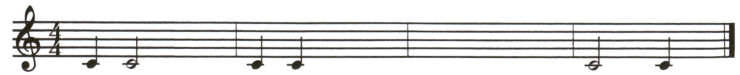

4. Complete each measure by adding just one **F** to each, so the counts add up to 4:

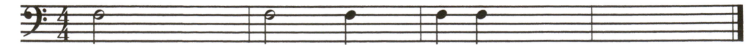

Assign with pages 12 & 13.

LIGHTLY ROW

1. Add BAR LINES like the first one shown, to divide the music into measures of 4 counts each.
2. Add a WHOLE REST in each measure to indicate silence for the LH or RH.
3. Write the name of each note in the box above it .
4. Play the piece.

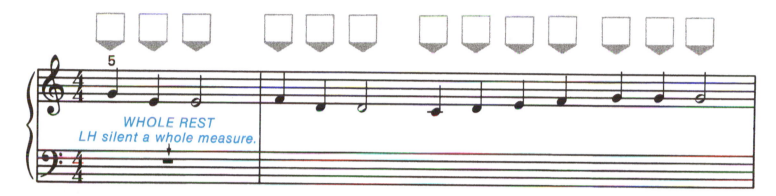

WHOLE REST
LH silent a whole measure.

RH silent a whole measure.

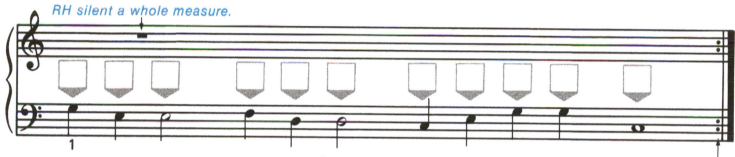

DOUBLE DOTS before DOUBLE BAR
mean repeat from the beginning.

AUNT RHODY

1. Add BAR LINES dividing the music into measures of the correct length.
2. Add WHOLE RESTS as needed.
3. Write the name of each note in the box above it.
4. Add something before the last DOUBLE BAR to indicate that the piece should be REPEATED.
5. Play the piece.

Assign with page 14.

Measuring Melodic 2nds & 3rds

Notes played **SEPARATELY** make a **MELODY**.
We call the intervals between these notes **MELODIC INTERVALS.**

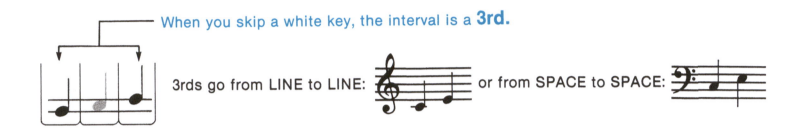

The distance from any white key to the next white key, up or down, is called a **2nd.**

2nds go from LINE to SPACE: or from SPACE to LINE:

When you skip a white key, the interval is a **3rd.**

3rds go from LINE to LINE: or from SPACE to SPACE:

1. Identify these intervals. If the interval moves UP, write UP in the top box. If it moves DOWN, write DOWN in the top box. Write the name of the interval in the lower box, as shown in the first 2 examples. If the note does not move up or down, write "SAME NOTE."

Assign with page 15.

Measuring Harmonic 2nds & 3rds

Notes played **TOGETHER** make **HARMONY**.
We call the intervals between these notes **HARMONIC INTERVALS.**

1. Play these HARMONIC **2nds** & **3rds.** Say the name of each interval as you play.

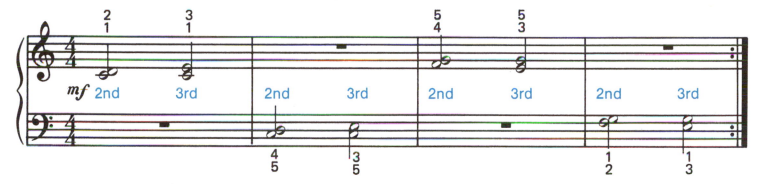

2. In the empty boxes, write the names of the notes that complete these HARMONIC INTERVALS:

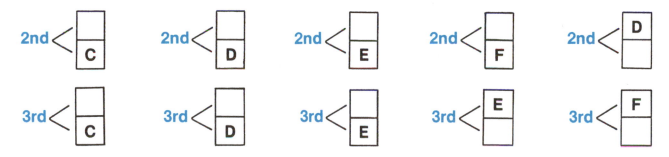

2nd < [ ] / C
2nd < [ ] / D
2nd < [ ] / E
2nd < [ ] / F
2nd < D / [ ]

3rd < [ ] / C
3rd < [ ] / D
3rd < [ ] / E
3rd < E / [ ]
3rd < F / [ ]

HARMONICA ROCK

3. Write the name of each harmonic interval in the box above it (2nd or 3rd).
4. Play, saying the name of each interval.

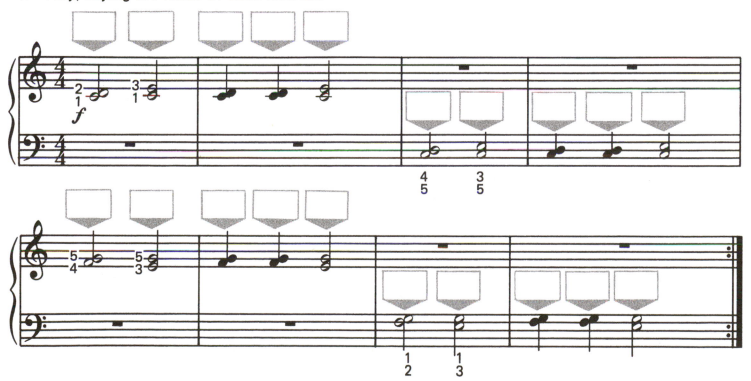

Assign with page 16.

Measuring Melodic 4ths & 5ths

When you skip 2 white keys, the interval is a **4th.**

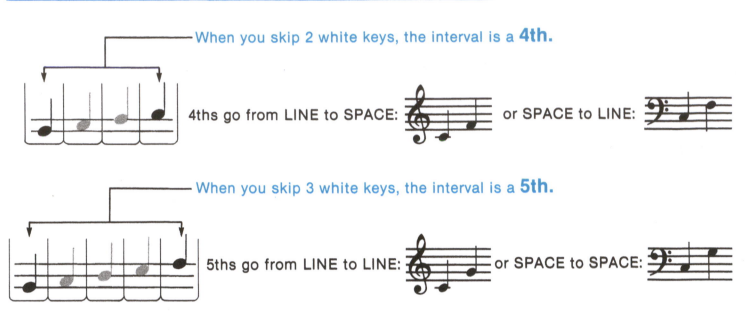

4ths go from LINE to SPACE: or SPACE to LINE:

When you skip 3 white keys, the interval is a **5th.**

5ths go from LINE to LINE: or SPACE to SPACE:

1. Write the names of the keys a 4th apart on this keyboard, beginning with the lowest F:

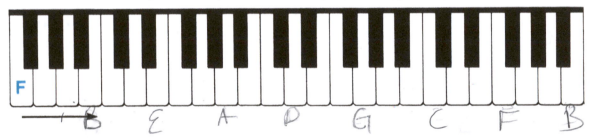

F → B E A D G C F B

2. Write the names of the keys a 5th apart on this keyboard, beginning with the lowest F:

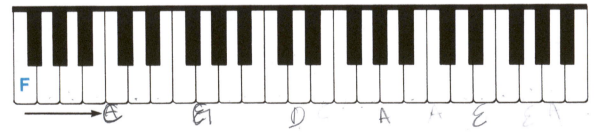

F → C G D A E B

3. Identify these intervals. If the interval moves UP, write UP in the top box. If it moves DOWN, write DOWN in the top box. Write the name of the interval in the lower box. If the note does not move up or down, write "SAME NOTE."

Measuring Harmonic 4ths & 5ths

1. Play these HARMONIC **4ths** & **5ths**. Listen to the sound of each interval.

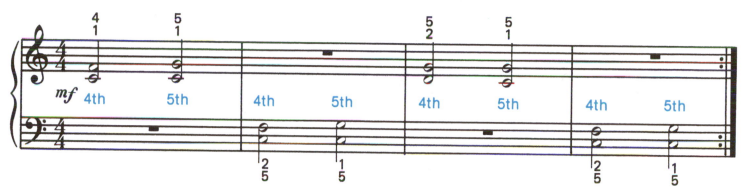

2. In the empty boxes, write the names of the notes that complete these HARMONIC INTERVALS:

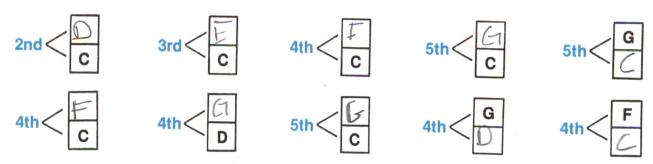

2nd: D / C
3rd: E / C
4th: F / C
5th: G / C
5th: G / C

4th: F / C
4th: G / D
5th: G / C
4th: G / D
4th: F / C

DUELING HARMONICS

3. Write the name of each harmonic interval in the box above it.
4. Play, saying the name of each interval.

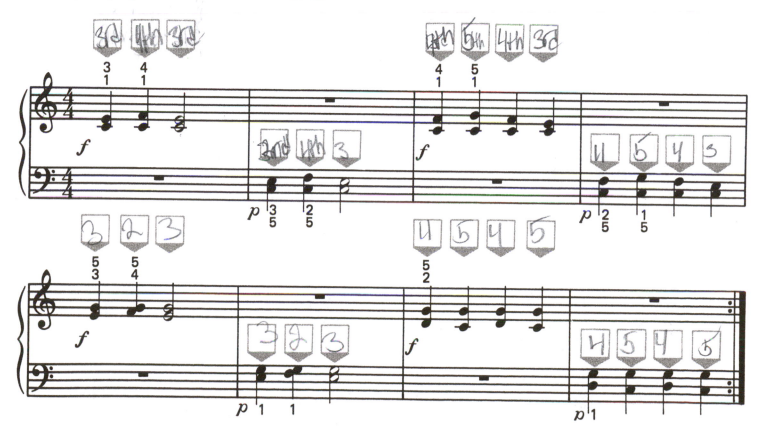

The C Major Chord

Assign with page 18.

The **C MAJOR CHORD** is made of three notes: **C E G.**

C is called the **ROOT** of the chord. The chord gets its letter-name from the ROOT.
E is called the **3rd** of the chord. It is a 3rd above the ROOT.
G is called the **5th** of the chord. It is a 5th above the ROOT.

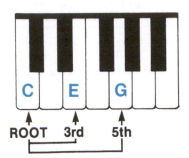

The C MAJOR CHORD may be played in every area of the keyboard.

1. Write as many C MAJOR CHORDS as you can on the following keyboard.
2. Play all the C MAJOR CHORDS you can find on the piano. Use LH 5 3 1 or RH 1 3 5.

Similarly, the **F MAJOR CHORD** may be formed using any **F** as the **ROOT**, and adding notes a **3rd** and a **5th** above.

3. Write as many F MAJOR CHORDS as you can on the following keyboard.
4. Play all the F MAJOR CHORDS you can find on the piano. Use LH 5 3 1 or RH 1 3 5.

Similarly, the **G MAJOR CHORD** may be formed using any **G** as the **ROOT**, and adding notes a **3rd** and a **5th** above.

5. Write as many G MAJOR CHORDS as you can on the following keyboard.
6. Play all the G MAJOR CHORDS you can find on your piano. Use LH 5 3 1 or RH 1 3 5.

The only chord you need to recognize on the bass & treble staffs now is the **C MAJOR CHORD!**

C MAJOR CHORD FOR LH.

7. Play & count.

C MAJOR CHORD FOR RH.

8. Play & count.

Reviewing Rests

RESTS ARE SIGNS OF SILENCE

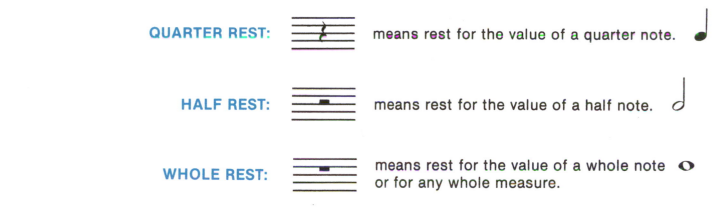

QUARTER REST: means rest for the value of a quarter note.

HALF REST: means rest for the value of a half note.

WHOLE REST: means rest for the value of a whole note or for any whole measure.

1. Trace the 2nd QUARTER REST, then draw 5 more.

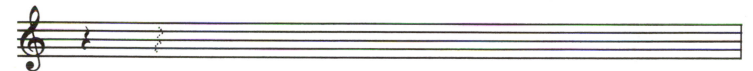

2. Fill in the 2nd HALF REST, then draw 5 more.
   The HALF REST sits on the 3rd line of the staff.

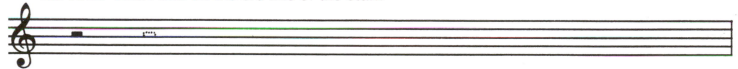

3. Fill in the 2nd WHOLE REST, then draw 5 more. The WHOLE REST hangs down from the 4th line.

4. Name these rests. Use Q for QUARTER, H for HALF, and W for WHOLE.

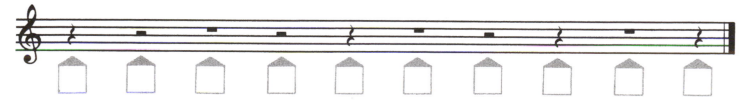

5. In the square below each rest, write the number of counts it receives in $\frac{4}{4}$ time.

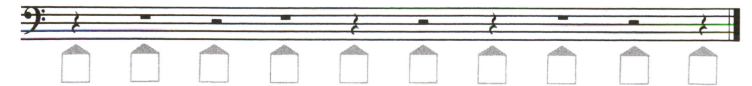

Introducing Ⓑ for Left Hand

Assign with page 20.

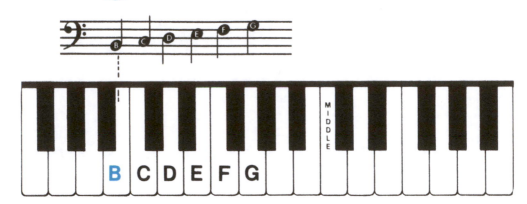

1. Write the name of each note in the box below it.

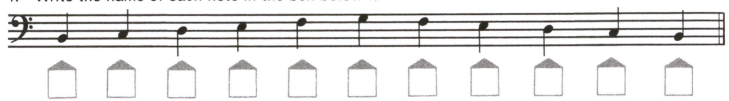

2. These notes are on **LINES.** Write the names in the boxes below.

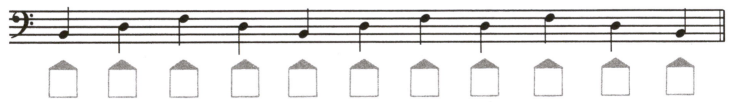

3. These notes are in **SPACES.** Write the names in the boxes.

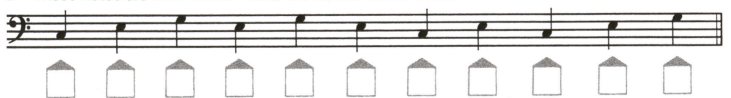

4. These notes are on **LINES & SPACES.** Write the names in the boxes.

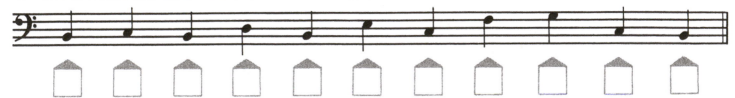

5. The notes in each of the following measures spell a word. Write the names in the boxes.

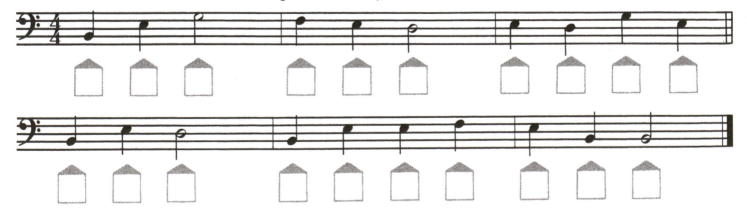

18

The G⁷ Chord for Left Hand

Assign with pages 20-21.

The construction of 7th chords will be more fully explained later. For now, the **G7 chord** will be made by playing **B F G** using LH 5 2 1. It is easy to move from the C MAJOR CHORD to the G7 CHORD and back again, because both chords have the same G in common.

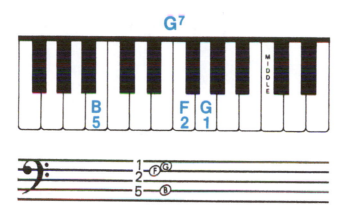

1. Practice changing from the **C** chord to **G7**.
   The COMMON TONE G is played by 1 in both chords!

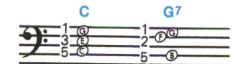

Chord Symbols

In popular music, CHORD SYMBOLS are used to identify chord names. The symbol for the C MAJOR CHORD is **C**. The symbol for the G SEVENTH CHORD is **G7**.

2. Write the chord symbols (C or G7) in the boxes below. Notice that a new symbol is used only when the chord changes.
3. Play and count.
4. Play and say the chord names.

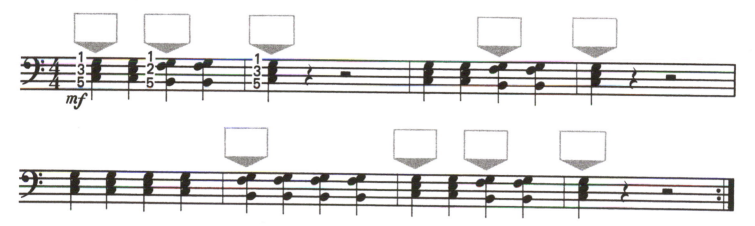

Tied Notes

When notes on the same line or space are joined with a curved line, we call them **TIED NOTES**.

5. Write the chord symbols in the boxes.
6. Play and count. Say chord names as you play.

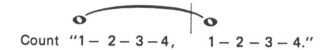

Count "1 − 2 − 3 − 4, 1 − 2 − 3 − 4."

Hold the key down for the **COMBINED VALUES OF BOTH NOTES!**

20

Introducing B for Right Hand

Assign with page 22.

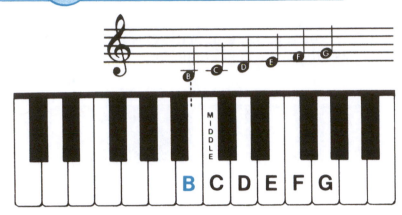

1. Write the name of each note in the box below it.

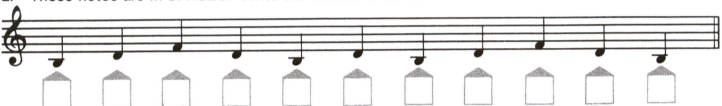

2. These notes are in **SPACES.** Write the names in the boxes below.

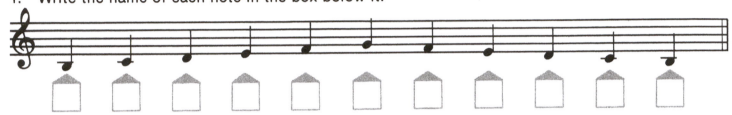

3. These notes are on **LINES.** Write the names in the boxes.

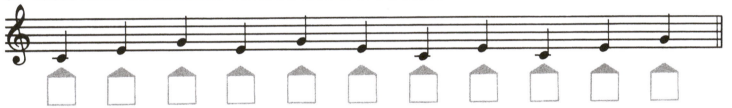

4. These notes are on **LINES & SPACES.** Write the names in the boxes.

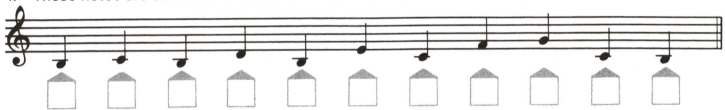

5. The notes in each of the following measures spell a word. Write the names in the boxes.

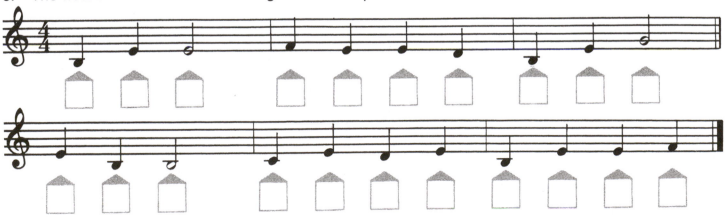

The G⁷ Chord for Right Hand

Assign with pages 22–23.

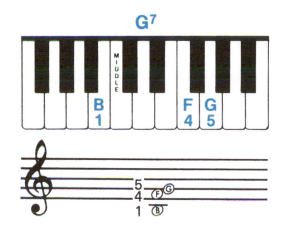

1. Practice changing from the **C** chord to **G⁷**.
   The COMMON TONE **G** is played by 5 in both chords!

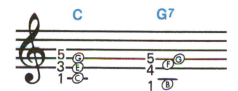

2. Write the chord symbols (C or G⁷) in the boxes below.
3. Play and count.
4. Play and say the chord names.

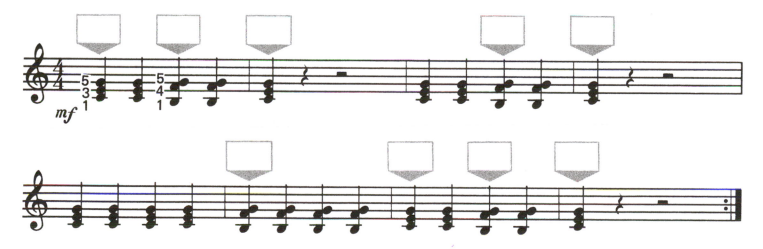

5. Write the correct symbols in the boxes below. Notice that when the GRAND STAFF (treble & bass staff together) is used, the chord symbols are written above the TREBLE staff.
6. Play & count. Say chord names as you play.

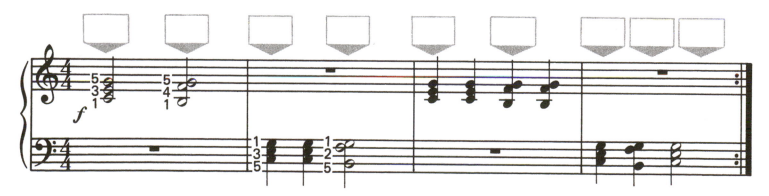

New Time Signature

3 = **3** beats to each measure.
4 = **QUARTER NOTE** gets ONE beat.

Dotted Half-Note

♩. **GETS 3 COUNTS**   COUNT: "1 - 2 - 3"

COUNT 2 for the HALF NOTE + 1 for the DOT!

1. In the box above each note, write the number of counts it receives.

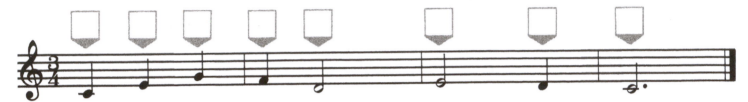

2. Check your answers. The notes in each measure of **3/4** time must add up to 3!

3. Under each line, write ONE NOTE equal in value to the sum of the TWO notes above it, as shown in the first example.

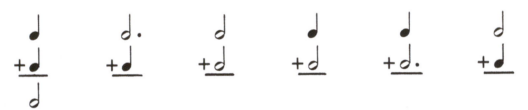

Reviewing Dynamics   DYNAMIC SIGNS show how **LOUD** or **SOFT** to play.

f (FORTE) = LOUD   *mf* (MEZZO FORTE) = MODERATELY LOUD   *p* (PIANO) = SOFT

---

4. Write the correct TIME SIGNATURE at the beginning of each of the following staffs.
5. Add CHORD SYMBOLS in the boxes above the treble staffs.
6. Play, carefully observing the dynamics.

    Notice that a WHOLE REST is used to show silence for a whole measure of **3/4** or **4/4** time!!

Moderately slow

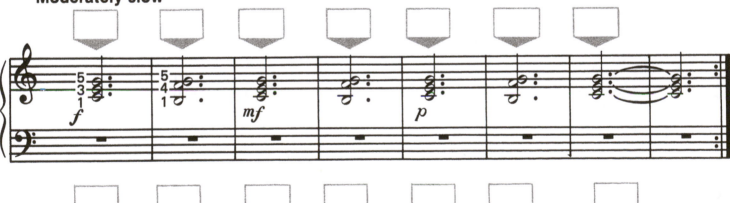

Slurs & Legato Playing

Assign with page 25.

> A **SLUR** is a curved line over or under notes on *different* lines or spaces.
>
> **SLURS** mean play **LEGATO** (smoothly connected).
>
> Slurs often divide the music into **PHRASES**. A **PHRASE** is a musical thought or sentence.

DAY IS DONE

1. Draw a slur over the notes that are played for the 2nd sentence of the lyrics.
2. Play the RH, counting aloud.
3. Play the RH again, saying or singing the words. Connect the notes of each phrase as smoothly as you can.
4. Add CHORD SYMBOLS in the boxes above the treble staffs.
5. Play with hands together.

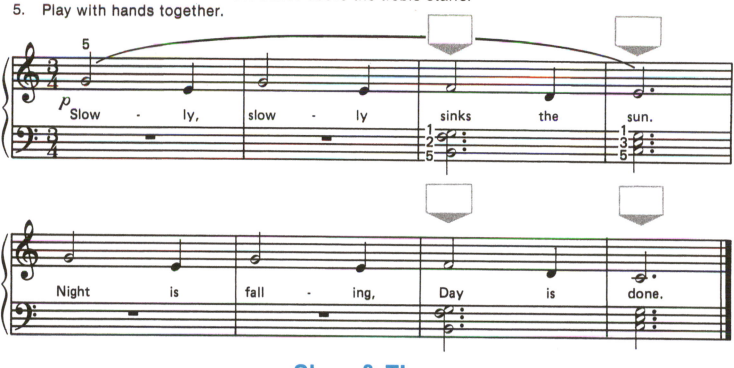

Slurs & Ties

If the notes are **DIFFERENT**—it's a **SLUR.**

Connect the notes, LEGATO!

If the notes are the **SAME**—it's a **TIE!**

Hold the notes, without repeating!

6. Write **TIE** or **SLUR** in the box under each pair of notes, as shown in the first box:

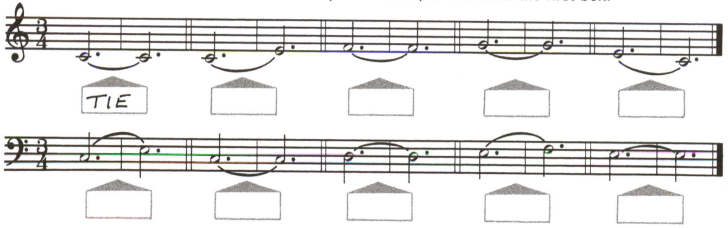

TIE

Introducing Ⓐ for Left Hand

Assign with page 26.

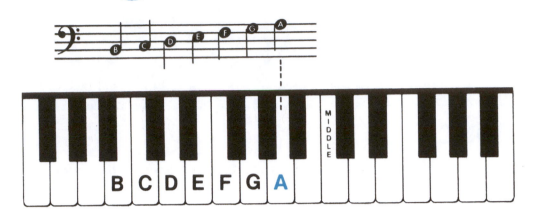

1. Write the name of each note in the box below it.

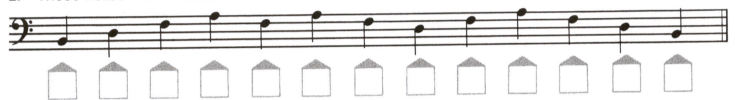

2. These notes are on **LINES.** Write the names in the boxes below.

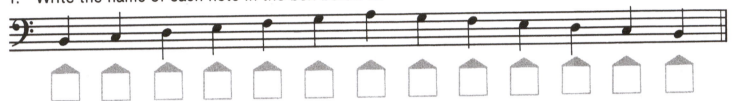

3. These notes are in **SPACES.** Write the names in the boxes.

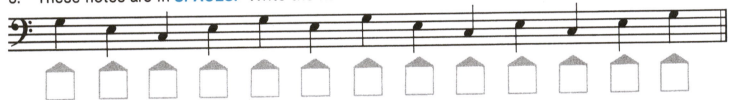

4. These notes are on **LINES & SPACES.** Write the names in the boxes.

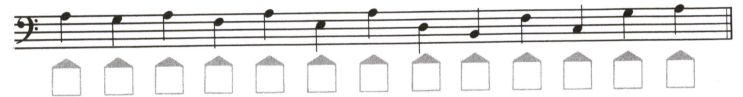

5. The notes in each of the following measures spell a word. Write the names in the boxes.

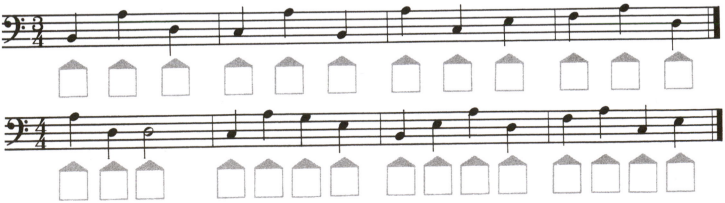

The F Major Chord for Left Hand

Assign with pages 26–27.

On page 16 of this book, you played the F MAJOR CHORD: **F A C.**
When moving from the C MAJOR CHORD to the F MAJOR CHORD, it is easier to play the F chord with the notes in this order: **C F A.** This allows the 5th finger to play C in both chords.

F MAJOR

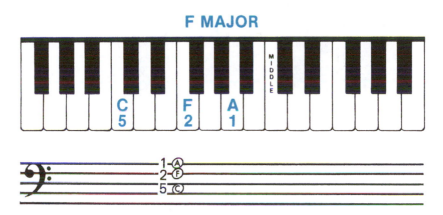

1. Practice changing from the C chord to the F chord.
   The COMMON TONE **C** is played by 5 in both chords.

2. Write the chord symbols (C, F or G7) in the boxes.
3. Play and count.   4. Play and say the chord names.

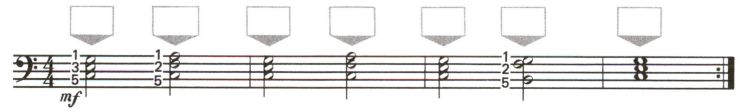

I'm Gonna Lay My Burden Down

Spiritual

This piece begins with an INCOMPLETE MEASURE of only 3 counts. The missing count is found in the LAST MEASURE!

5. Write the chord symbol in the box above each chord.
6. Play and count. Notice that the last incomplete measure plus the 1st incomplete measure makes one COMPLETE measure when you make the repeat.
7. Play and say the chord names.   8. Play and say or sing the words.

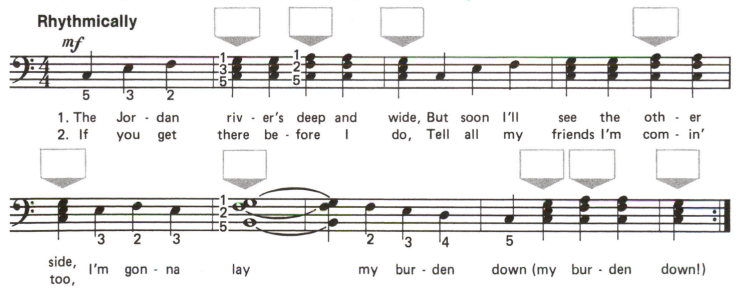

Introducing Ⓐ for Right Hand

Assign with page 28.

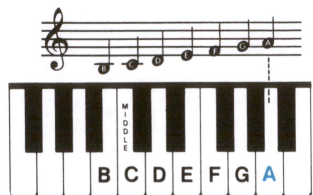

1. Write the name of each note in the box below it.

2. These notes are in **SPACES.** Write the names in the boxes below.

3. These notes are on **LINES.** Write the names in the boxes.

4. These notes are on **LINES & SPACES.** Write the names in the boxes.

5. The notes in each of the following measures spell a word. Write the names in the boxes.

The F Major Chord for Right Hand

Assign with pages 28-29.

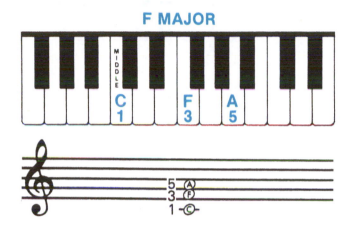

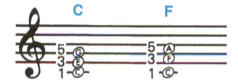

1. Practice changing from the C chord to the F chord.
   The COMMON TONE **C** is played by **1** in both chords!

2. Write the chord symbols (C, F or G⁷) in the boxes below.
3. Play and count.
4. Play and say the chord names.

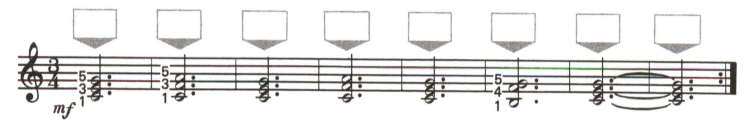

WALTZING CHORDS

5. Write the chord symbols in the boxes below.
6. Play and count.
7. Play, saying the chord name each time the chord changes.

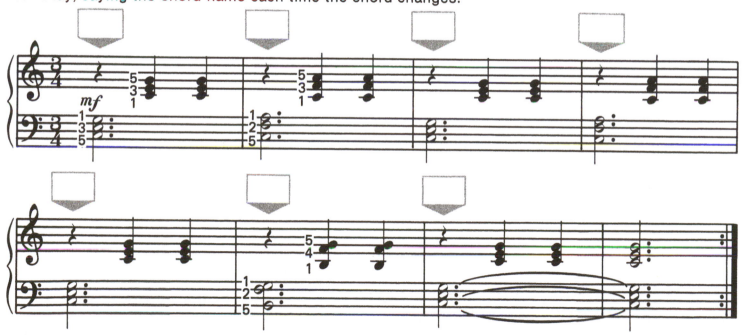

28

Assign with page 30.

G Position

RH 1 on the G above middle C.

LH 5 on the G below middle C.

THE BAND-LEADER

1. Write the names of the notes in the boxes.   2. Play.

Moderately fast, like a march

f I'm the lead-er of the band. Out in front I proud-ly stand.

All I do is wave my hand; Out comes mu-sic loud and grand!

3. Write notes from the G POSITION that spell these words. The note values in each measure must add up to 4 counts. Turn note-stems DOWN when notes are ON or ABOVE the middle line of either staff. Turn note-stems UP when notes are BELOW the middle line.

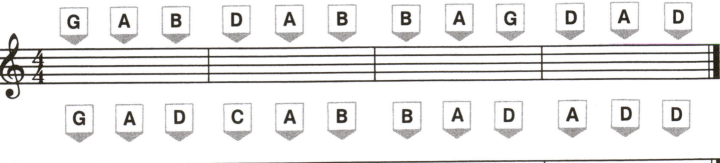

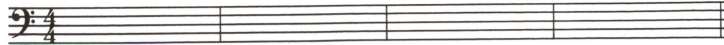

| G | A | B | D | A | B | B | A | G | D | A | D |

| G | A | D | C | A | B | B | A | D | A | D | D |

Melodic Intervals in G Position

1. Write the names of the notes in the boxes above the staffs.
2. Write the names of the intervals in the boxes below the staffs.

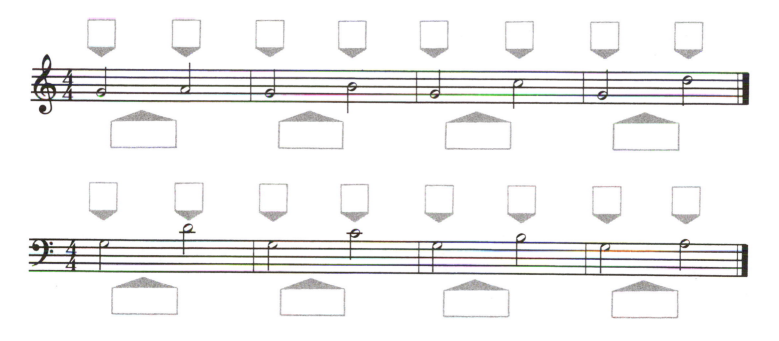

Harmonic Intervals in G Position

3. Write the names of the notes in the boxes above the staffs. Write the name of the lower note in the lower box and the name of the higher note in the higher box.
4. Write the names of the intervals in the boxes below the staffs.

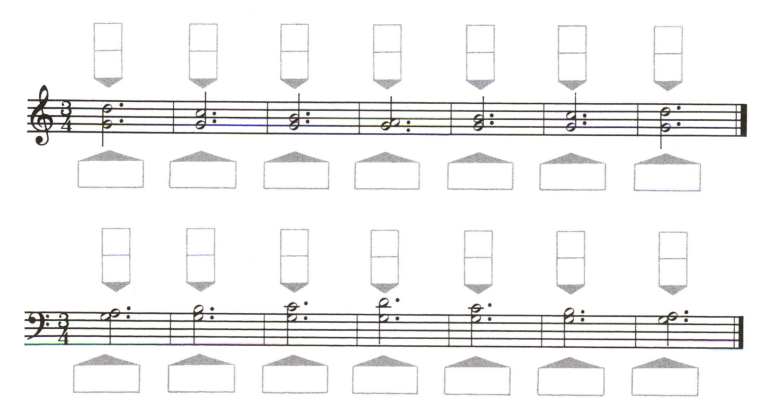

The Sharp Sign

Assign with page 33.

The **SHARP SIGN** ♯ before a note means play the next key to the right, whether black or white.

1. Make some SHARP SIGNS:

First, draw the two vertical lines.

Then, add the heavy slanting lines.

Draw 4 sharp signs here:

2. Write the names of the ♯ keys in the boxes below.

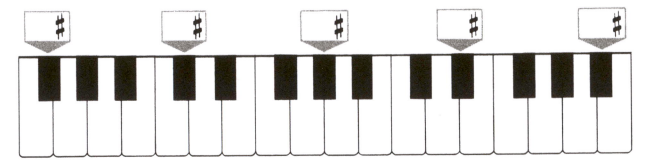

3. Change each of the notes below to a sharp note. Write the sharp sign BEFORE the note!

    When writing sharp signs, be sure the **CENTER** of the sign is on the line or space of the note to be sharped:

4. Write the name of each note in the box above it.

5. Play the notes, using RH 3 or LH 3.

The G Major & D⁷ Chords for Left Hand

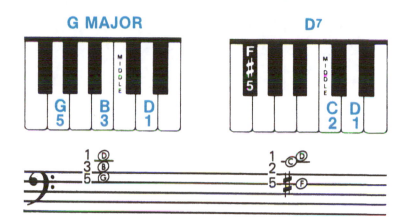

1. Practice changing from the G chord to the D⁷ chord.
   The COMMON TONE **D** is played by 1 in both chords.

2. Write the chord symbols (G or D⁷) in the boxes below.
3. Play and count.   4. Play and say the chord names.

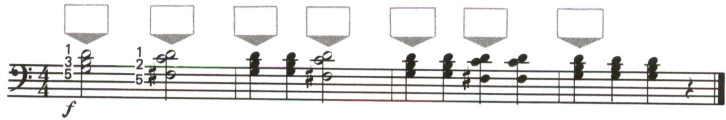

LIZA JANE

5. Write the chord symbols in the boxes below.
6. Play and count.   7. Play and sing or say the words.

Folk Song

Moderately fast

N.C. (no chord)

1. Got   a   gal   in   Bal - ti - more;   Li'l Li - za   Jane!
2. If   my Li - za   you should see;

N.C.

Four - teen kids, ex - pec - tin' more;   Li'l Li - za   Jane!
Send her   to   me   C. O. D.;

Assign with page 36.

The G Major & D⁷ Chords for Right Hand

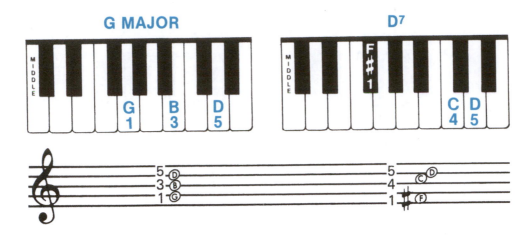

1. Practice changing from the **G** chord to **D⁷**.
   The COMMON TONE **D** is played by 5 in both chords.

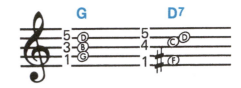

2. Write the chord symbols (G or D⁷) in the boxes below.
3. Play and count.   4. Play and say the chord names.

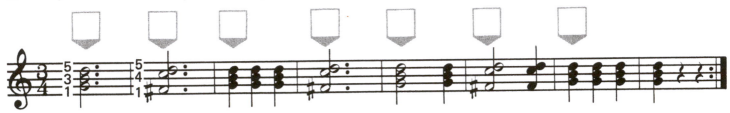

Block Chords & Broken Chords

BLOCK CHORDS: Notes are stacked VERTICALLY.
All notes are played TOGETHER.

G MAJOR & D⁷ BLOCK CHORDS:

BROKEN CHORDS: Notes occur HORIZONTALLY,
and are played SEPARATELY.

G MAJOR & D⁷ BROKEN CHORDS:

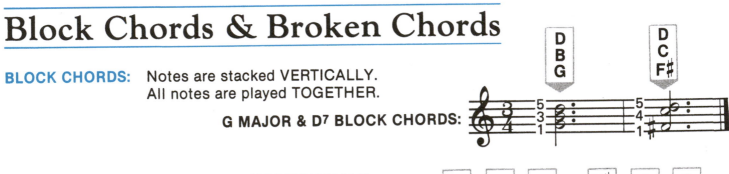

5. Write the names of the individual chord notes in the boxes below.

6. Write BLOCK or BROKEN under each chord.
7. Play the chords with the LH.

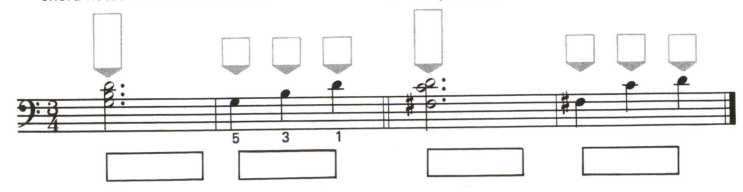

The Damper Pedal

Assign with page 37.

Use the RIGHT FOOT on the RIGHT PEDAL, called the **DAMPER PEDAL.**

This sign shows when the damper pedal is to be used:

Pedal down   Hold pedal   Pedal up

1. Write the chord symbols in the boxes below.
2. Play and count, using the DAMPER PEDAL as indicated.
   LISTEN to the effect produced by the pedal, which causes all the notes of each line to blend in a continous sound!

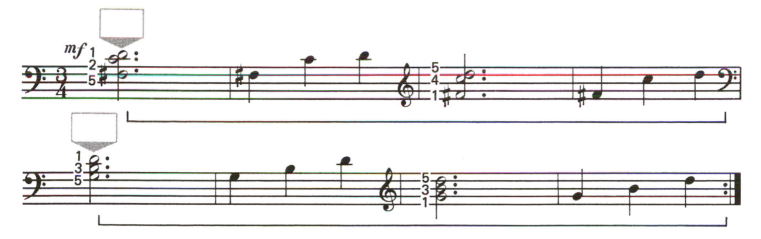

3. In the blank measure following each BLOCK CHORD below, write the notes of the same chord BROKEN.
4. Write the names of the individual chord notes in the boxes.
5. Draw a long PEDAL SIGN under each line. (Use the 2 lines above as examples.)
6. Play, using the pedal as indicated. LISTEN!

Moderately slow

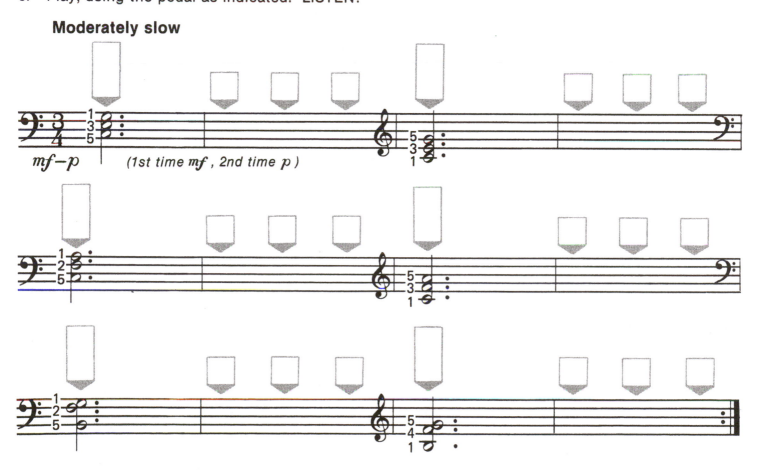

mf – p   (1st time *mf* , 2nd time *p*)

Introducing Ⓔ for Left Hand

Assign with page 38.

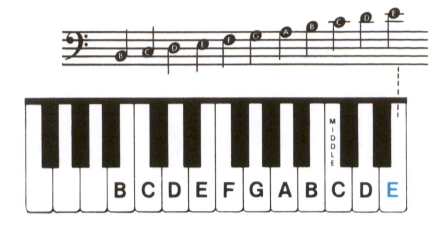

This reviews all LH notes studied so far!

1. Write the name of each note in the box below it.

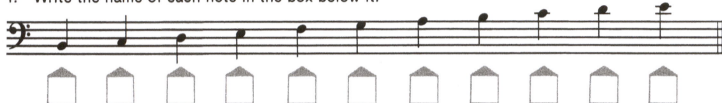

2. These notes are on **LINES.** Write the names in the boxes below.

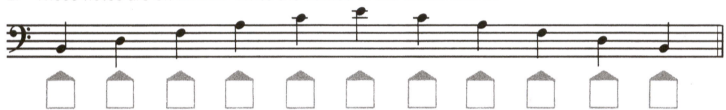

3. These notes are in **SPACES.** Write the names in the boxes.

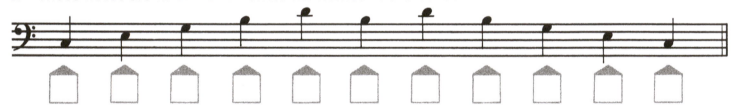

4. These notes are on **LINES & SPACES.** Write the names in the boxes.

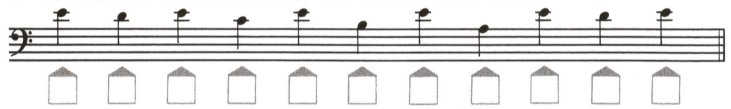

5. The notes in each **PAIR** of measures spell a word. Write the names in the boxes.

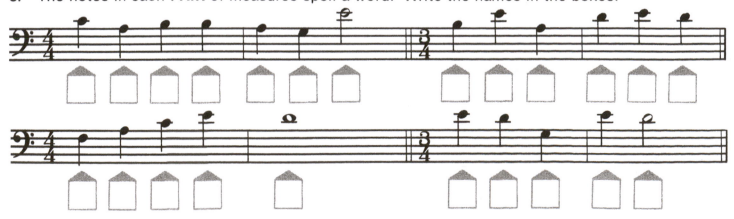

New C Major Chord Position for Left Hand

You have learned that the C MAJOR CHORD contains the notes **C E G.**
When moving from the G MAJOR CHORD to the C MAJOR chord, it is easier to play the C chord with
the notes in this order: **G C E.** This allows the 5th finger to play G in both chords.

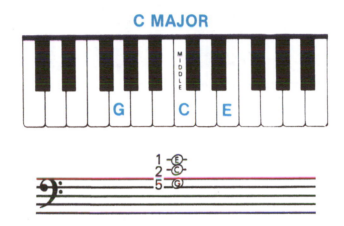

1. Practice changing from the G chord to the C chord.
   The COMMON TONE **G** is played by 5 in both chords.

2. Write the chord symbols (G, C or D7) in the boxes below.
3. Play and count.
4. Play and say the chord names.

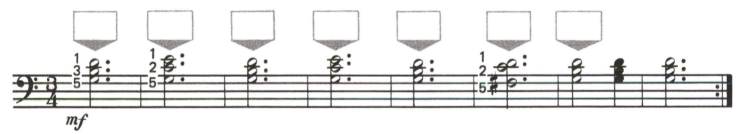

BROKEN CHORDS may be played several ways. Each note may be played separately, or one note may
be played, followed by the remaining 2 notes.

5. Write the chord symbols in the boxes below. You will have to look at all the notes in each measure
   to determine the chord name.
6. Play and say the chord names.

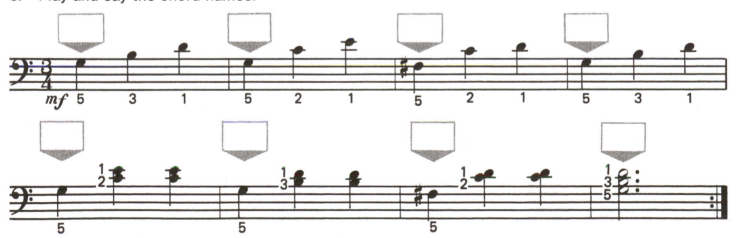

Introducing E for Right Hand

Assign with page 40.

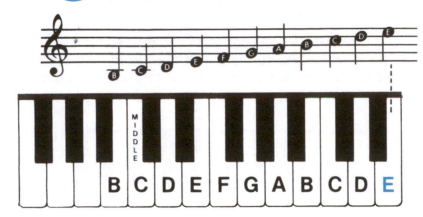

This reviews all
RH notes
studied so far!

1. Write the name of each note in the boxes below.

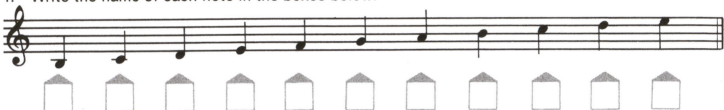

2. These notes are in **SPACES.** Write the names in the boxes below.

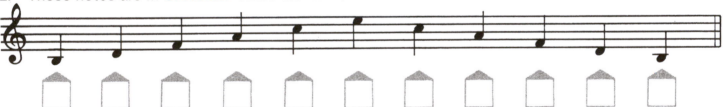

3. These notes are on **LINES.** Write the names in the boxes.

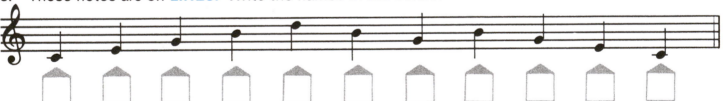

4. These notes are on **LINES & SPACES.** Write the names in the boxes.

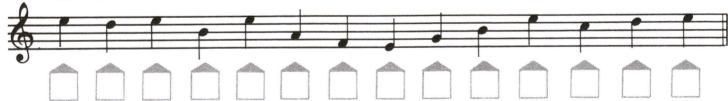

5. The notes in each PAIR of measures spell a word. Write the names in the boxes.

New C Major Chord Position—Right Hand

C MAJOR

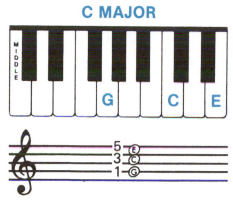

1. Practice changing from the G chord to the C chord.
   The COMMON TONE **G** is played by 1 in both chords.

In this piece both hands always play the same chords at the same time.
In the RH, the chords are BROKEN. The LH plays BLOCK chords.

2. Write the chord symbols in the boxes.
3. Play. Carefully observe all ties and pedal indications.

Moderately slow

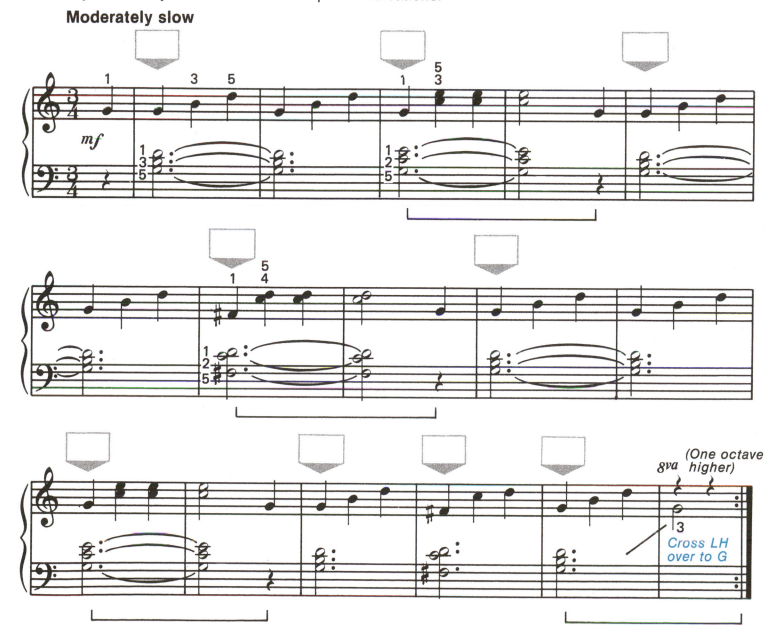

(One octave *8va* higher)

Cross LH over to G

Middle C Position

Assign with pages 42–43.

In the MIDDLE C POSITION, both thumbs are on middle C!
No new notes are used!

NEW DYNAMIC SIGNS:

CRESCENDO
(gradually louder)

DIMINUENDO
(gradually softer)

PRELUDE ON MIDDLE C

1. Write the note names in the boxes.
2. Play.

Getting Ready for Eighth Notes

Assign with page 44.

This piece will prepare you to play EIGHT NOTES.

1. Play at a very moderate speed. Count aloud, very evenly.
   The sign ⌒ over the G in the 6th measure is a FERMATA or "Hold" sign. Hold the note longer than its value. (Approximately *twice* its value is a good general rule.)
2. Play again, saying or singing the words.

SHOO, FLY, SHOO!

Fly's a - buzz - in', Shoo, fly, shoo! Fly's a - buzz - in', Shoo, fly, shoo!

Fly's a - buzz - in', Shoo, fly, shoo! Don't buzz 'round my dar - lin'!

Eighth Notes

Assign with page 45.

Two eighth notes are played in the time of **one quarter note.**

To count music containing eighth notes, divide each beat into 2 parts:

count: **"1 · &"** or **"quar · ter"** for each quarter note;
count: **"1 · &"** or **"2 · 8ths"** for each pair of eighth notes.

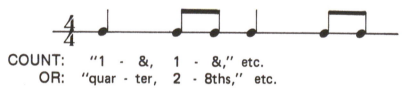

COUNT: "1 - &, 1 - &," etc.
OR: "quar - ter, 2 - 8ths," etc.

1. Play at the same speed you played SHOO, FLY, SHOO! Count aloud.
2. Play again, saying or singing the words.

SKIP TO MY LOU!

Lost my part - ner, Skip to my Lou! Lost my part - ner, Skip to my Lou!

Lost my part - ner, Skip to my Lou! Skip to my Lou, my dar - lin'!

Assign with pages 48–49.

Introducing Dotted Quarter Notes

A DOT INCREASES THE LENGTH OF A NOTE BY ONE HALF ITS VALUE.

QUARTER NOTE: **DOTTED QUARTER NOTE:**

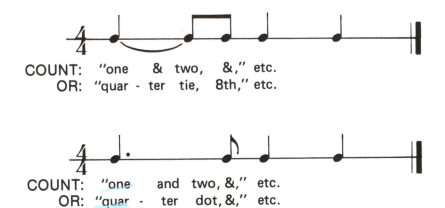

The DOTTED QUARTER NOTE is usually followed by a SINGLE EIGHTH NOTE, written:

HERE ARE TWO DIFFERENT WAYS OF WRITING THE SAME RHYTHM:

COUNT: "one   & two, &," etc.
OR: "quar - ter tie, 8th," etc.

COUNT: "one   and two, &," etc.
OR: "quar - ter dot, &," etc.

1. In the following line, draw the TIES as indicated.
2. Play & count.
3. Play and sing or say the words.

Moderately slow

1. Sleep,   my child, and   peace   at-tend thee,   All   through   the   night;
2. Guard - ian an - gels   God   will send thee,   All   through   the   night.

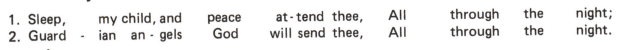

4. In the following line, some quarter notes need dots after them. Add the correct dots to make the rhythm the same as on the line above.
5. Play & count. This line should sound exactly the same as the one above!

Measuring 6ths

Assign with pages 52–55.

When you skip 4 white keys, the interval is a **6th.**

6ths go from LINE to SPACE: or SPACE to LINE:

1. Write the names of the keys a 6th apart on this keyboard, beginning with the lowest C:

C   A   F   D   B   G   E

2. Write the names of these MELODIC intervals in the boxes.

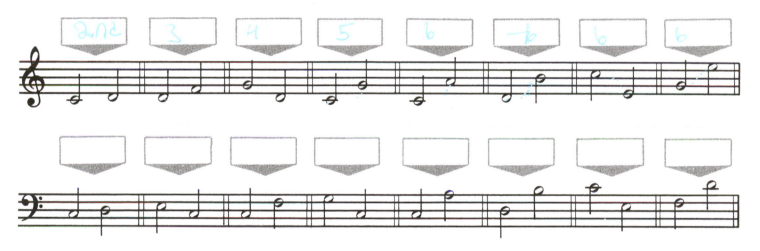

2nd	3	4	5	6	7	6	6

3. Write the names of these HARMONIC intervals in the boxes.

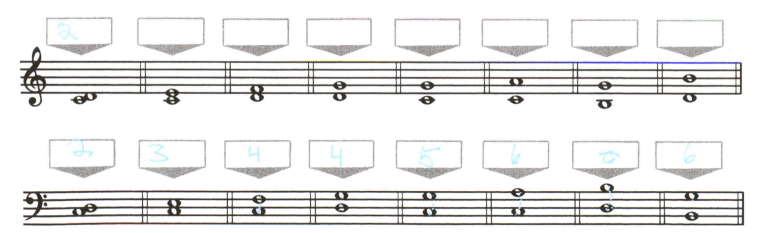

2							

2	3	4	4	5	6	6	6

Assign with pages 56–57.

Moving Up & Down the Keyboard in 6ths

1. In each measure below, add a whole note a 6th ABOVE each of the following notes.
    Say the names of the notes as you write them.

2. Play, using RH 1–5 on each 6th.

3. In each measure below, add a whole note a 6th BELOW each of the following notes.
    Say the names of the notes as you write them.

4. Play, using LH 5–1 on each 6th.

Moving Around the Keyboard in 6ths

1. In each measure below, add a note a 6th ABOVE each of the following notes.
    Say the names.

2. Play, using RH 1–5 on each 6th.

3. In each measure below, add a note a 6th BELOW each of the following notes.
    Say the names.

4. Play, using LH 5–1 on each 6th.

5. Play the 2 lines as one complete piece.

Motawski Sarah   S Sarah Motawski

Measuring 7ths & Octaves

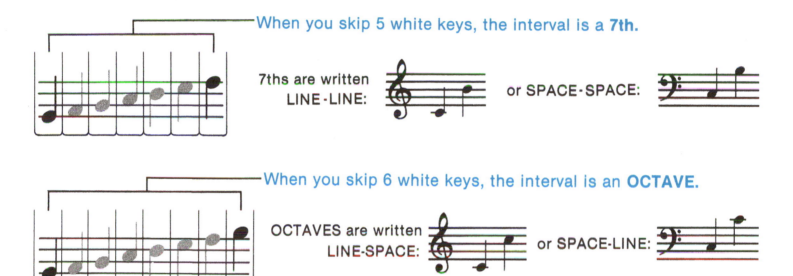

When you skip 5 white keys, the interval is a 7th.

7ths are written LINE-LINE: or SPACE-SPACE:

When you skip 6 white keys, the interval is an OCTAVE.

OCTAVES are written LINE-SPACE: or SPACE-LINE:

1. In each measure below, add a higher half note to make the indicated MELODIC interval.
2. Play. Use RH 1–5 or LH 5–1 on the 5th, 6th, 7th, & OCTAVE.

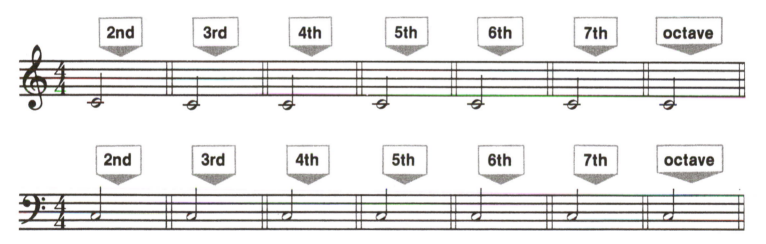

| 2nd | 3rd | 4th | 5th | 6th | 7th | octave |

| 2nd | 3rd | 4th | 5th | 6th | 7th | octave |

3. In each measure below, add a WHOLE NOTE directly above the given note to make the indicated HARMONIC interval.
4. Play. Use RH 1–5 or LH 5–1 on each interval.

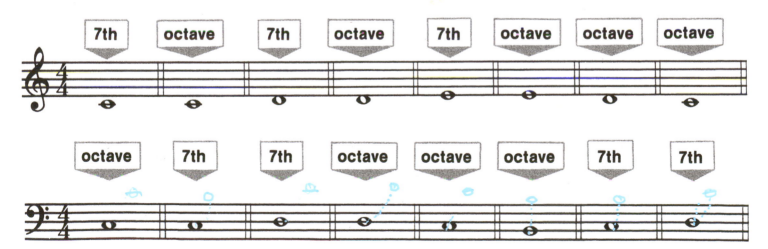

| 7th | octave | 7th | octave | 7th | octave | octave | octave |

| octave | 7th | 7th | octave | octave | octave | 7th | 7th |

The Flat Sign

Assign with page 60.

The **FLAT SIGN** ♭ before a note means play the next key to the **LEFT**, whether black or white.

1. Make some FLAT SIGNS:

   First, draw one vertical line.
   Then add the heavier curved line.

   Draw 4 flat signs here.

2. Write the names of the ♭ keys in the boxes below.

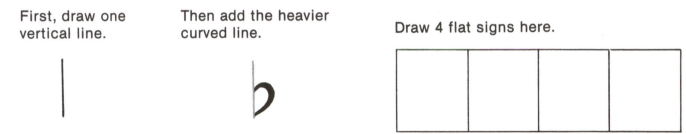

3. Change each of the notes below to a flat note. Write the flat sign **BEFORE** the note!

   When writing flat signs, be sure to **CENTER** the flat sign on the line or space of the note to be flatted:

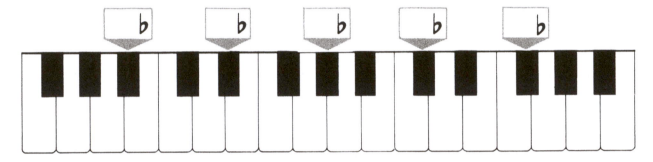

4. Write the name of each note in the box above it.
5. Play the notes. Using RH 3 or LH 3.

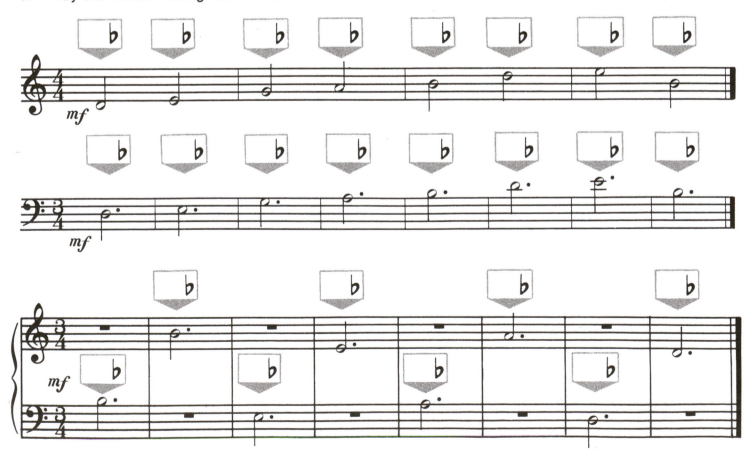

Half Steps

A **HALF STEP** is the distance from any key to the very next key above or below, whether black or white. **NO KEY BETWEEN.**

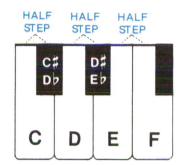

Whole Steps

A **WHOLE STEP** is equal to 2 half steps. Skip one key . . . black or white. **ONE KEY BETWEEN.**

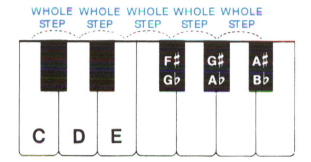

1. In the following squares write ½ for each HALF STEP and 1 for each WHOLE STEP indicated by the arrows.

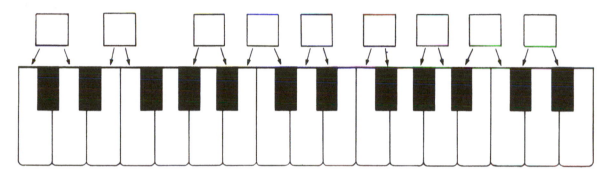

Tetrachords

A **TETRACHORD** is a series of **FOUR NOTES** having a pattern of **WHOLE STEP, WHOLE STEP, HALF STEP.**

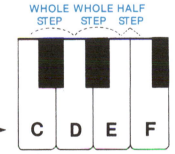

The notes of a tetrachord must be in alphabetical order —→

2. Study the following 2 TETRACHORDS and answer these questions:
   - Does each consist of WHOLE STEP, WHOLE STEP, HALF STEP? Answer: _____.
   - Are the notes of each tetrachord NEIGHBORING LETTERS OF THE MUSICAL ALPHABET? Answer: _____
   - Underline the correct spelling of the **D** tetrachord: **D E G♭ G   D E F♯ G**

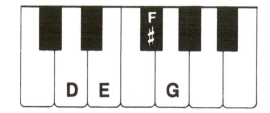

The Major Scale

Assign with pages 62-63.

> The **MAJOR SCALE** is made of **TWO TETRACHORDS** *joined* by a **WHOLE STEP**.

1. Write the letter names of the notes of the C MAJOR SCALE on the keyboard below. Use the tetrachord patterns, and be sure each whole step and half step is correct!

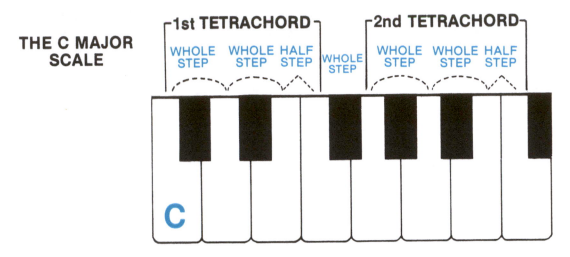

2. Complete the tetrachord beginning on C. Write one note over each finger number.

3. Complete the tetrachord beginning on G. Write one note under each finger number.

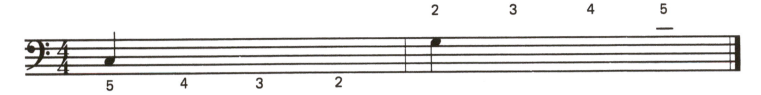

4. Play the above. Use LH on the 1st tetrachord and RH on the 2nd tetrachord.

5. Complete a tetrachord beginning on each of the notes below. Write one note under each finger number.

6. Play with RH. By crossing 1 under 3, you can play the entire scale of 8 notes with the 5 fingers of one hand!

7. Complete a tetrachord beginning on each of the notes below. Write one note over each finger number.

8. Play with LH. Cross 3 over 1.

9. Play each of the above 2 scales again, beginning on the HIGHEST note, and descending to the LOWEST. (Read the notes and fingering in REVERSE, from right to left!) Play the 1st with RH, crossing 3 over 1, and the 2nd with LH, crossing 1 under 3.

Triads

Assign with page 64.

A TRIAD IS A 3-NOTE CHORD.

MAJOR CHORDS (such as C E G, F A C, G B D) are examples of TRIADS.
SEVENTH CHORDS are not considered to be TRIADS. You will learn later that these are really 4-note chords with one note purposely omitted.

THE THREE NOTES OF A TRIAD ARE:

The ROOT is the note from which the triad gets its name. The ROOT of a C triad is C.

> To build a triad, measure the 3rd and the 5th upward from the ROOT.
> When a triad is in ROOT POSITION (with the root at the bottom),
> *all* the notes of the triad will be on LINES, or *all* of them will be in SPACES.

1. Build triads using each of the following LINE NOTES as the root.

2. Build triads using each of the following SPACE NOTES as the root.

3. Play the triads on the 2 staffs above, using RH 1 3 5. Name each triad as you play.
   The TRIAD name is the same as the ROOT name.

4. Build triads using each of the following LINE NOTES as the root.

5. Build triads using each of the following SPACE NOTES as the root.

6. Play the triads on the 2 staffs above, using LH 5 3 1. Name each triad as you play.

The "Triad Vocabulary"

Assign with page 65.

When you name the notes of any **TRIAD IN ROOT POSITION,** you will always skip **ONE** letter of the musical alphabet between each note. The triads you played on the previous page are:

CEG   DFA   EGB   FAC   GBD   ACE   BDF

This is the complete **"TRIAD VOCABULARY!"** It should be memorized!

Triad Puzzle

If you have memorized the TRIAD VOCABULARY, the puzzle below can be solved very quickly. This puzzle will help you test your knowledge of the vocabulary.

1. Cover up the TRIAD VOCABULARY above.
2. Fill in the puzzle with TRIADS in root position, using the given letter name as the root.
    If you make a mistake you will soon know it because the puzzle will not work!

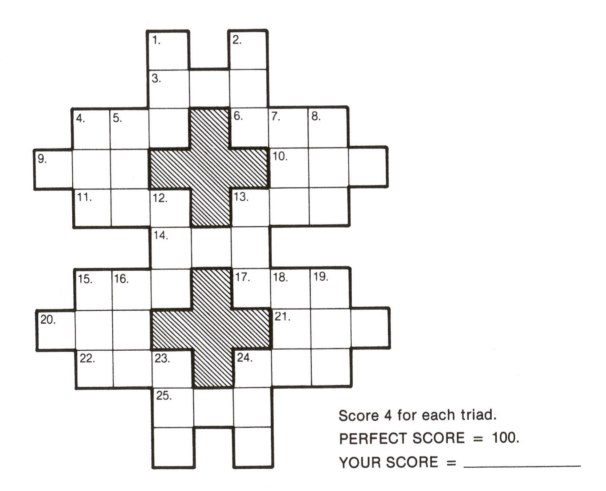

Score 4 for each triad.
PERFECT SCORE = 100.
YOUR SCORE = _____

ACROSS

3. A	11. C	20. G
4. F	13. D	21. E
6. G	14. B	22. D
9. F	15. G	24. E
10. D	17. A	25. C

DOWN

1. F	8. D	18. C
2. C	12. G	19. E
4. F	13. D	23. A
5. A	15. G	24. E
7. B	16. B	

The Primary Triads

Assign with page 66.

Music based on the C major scale is said to be in the KEY OF C MAJOR.

The **PRIMARY TRIADS** of any key are built on the 1st, 4th, & 5th notes of the scale.

The chords are identified by the Roman numerals, **I, IV, & V** (1, 4, & 5).

In the key of C major, the **I CHORD** (1 CHORD) is the C TRIAD.
The **IV CHORD** (4 CHORD) is the F TRIAD.
The **V CHORD** (5 CHORD) is the G TRIAD.

THE PRIMARY TRIADS IN C MAJOR in the bass clef:

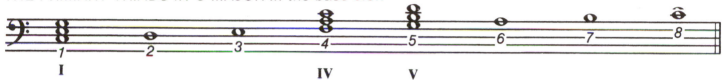

1. Build the PRIMARY TRIADS IN C MAJOR in the treble clef. Add two notes to the 1st, 4th, and 5th notes of the scale to complete the triads.

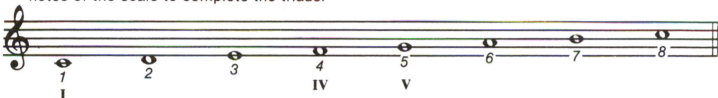

The V⁷ Chord

To make a 7th CHORD, a note an interval of a 7th above the root is added to a TRIAD.

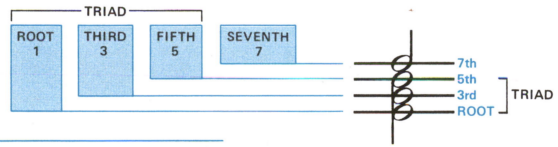

The Primary Chords

As a **GENERAL RULE,** the **V⁷** (called "5-7") chord is used instead of the V triad.

The **V⁷** chord is not a triad, since it has 4 notes instead of 3. We therefore call the **I CHORD, IV CHORD** and the **V⁷ CHORD** the PRIMARY **CHORDS,** rather than the PRIMARY **TRIADS.**

THE PRIMARY CHORDS IN C MAJOR in the bass clef:

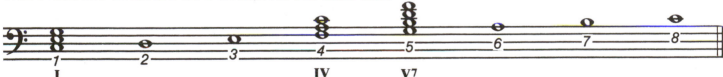

2. Build the PRIMARY CHORDS IN C MAJOR in the treble clef. 1st build TRIADS on **I, IV, & V,** then add to the V triad a note that is a 7th above the root, to make a **V⁷** chord.

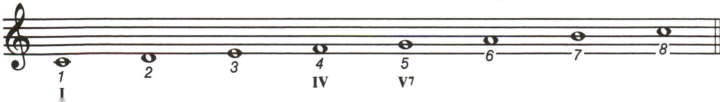

50

About Chord Progressions

Assign with pages 66-67.

When we change from one chord to another, we call this a "CHORD PROGRESSION."
When all chords are in root position, the hand must LEAP from one chord to the next.

To avoid leaps, and to make smooth progressions:

In the **IV** chord, the 5th (C) is moved down an octave.

In the **V7** chord, the 5th (D) is omitted. The 3rd (B) & 7th (F) are moved down an octave.

The progression **I IV I V7 I** is now much easier to play, and it sounds smoother.
Note that there is a COMMON TONE between each neighboring pair of chords:

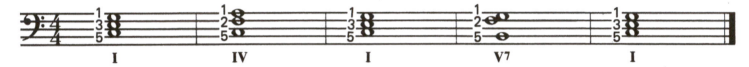

1. Play the top line of this page.
2. Play the line immediately above. Compare.

About Key Signatures

Music based on any particular scale is said to be in the KEY of that scale. If there are sharps or flats in the scale, they are shown at the beginning of the music, just after the clef sign. These sharps or flats make up the KEY SIGNATURE, and remain in effect throughout the music, or until a new signature is given.

Since the C MAJOR SCALE has NO SHARPS & NO FLATS, music written in the KEY OF C MAJOR is said to have a KEY SIGNATURE of NO sharps and NO flats!

REVIEW: THE PRIMARY CHORDS IN C MAJOR

KEY OF C MAJOR
Key Signature: no ♯, no ♭.

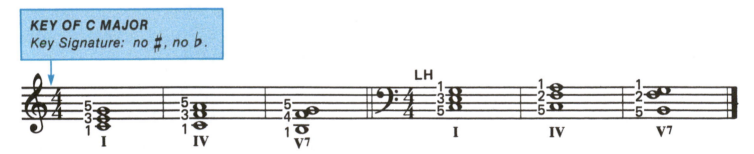

3. Write the PRIMARY CHORDS in the KEY OF C MAJOR, using the above positions.
4. Play. Say "One chord, four chord, five-seventh chord" as you play.

Completing the Grand Staff

Assign with pages 68–69.
(Prepares for page 70.)

With the introduction of 4 new notes, low G & A in the bass staff and high F & G in the treble staff, you have now covered all the notes of the GRAND STAFF!

This page will help you to learn these new notes, and will review all of the old ones.

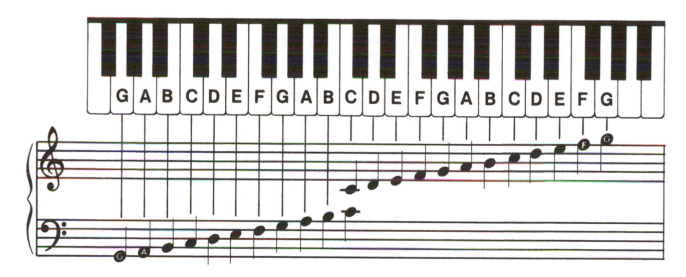

Some students use "memory devices," such as the following.

| **BASS CLEF** | *Lines:* | "**G**ood **B**oys **D**o **F**ine **A**lways." | *Spaces:* | "**A**ll **C**ars **E**at **G**as." |
| **TREBLE CLEF** | *Lines:* | "**E**very **G**ood **B**oy **D**oes **F**ine." | *Spaces:* | "**F A C E**." |

If you have completed all the pages leading up to this one, you will have no need to use these devices, which really slow down the note-reading process. It is better to recognize the notes on the staff immediately than to have to "count up" lines or spaces. The best readers recognize the individual notes, but read mostly by INTERVAL from note to note, once the basic position is located on the keyboard.

1. These notes are on **LINES.** Write the names in the boxes.

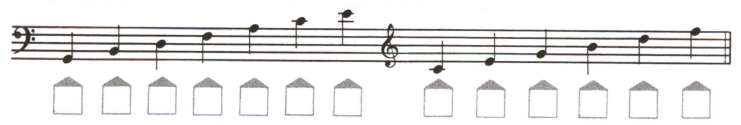

2. These notes are in **SPACES.** Write the names in the boxes.

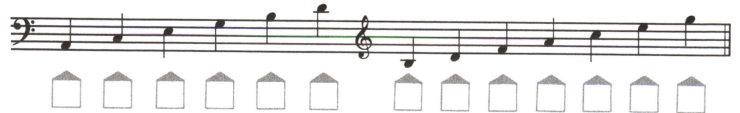

3. These notes are on **LINES & SPACES.** Write the names in the boxes.

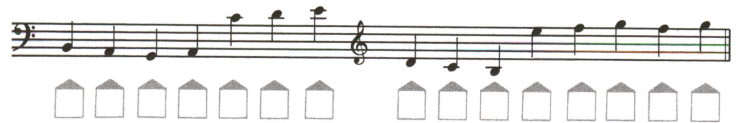

The Key of G Major

Assign with page 70.

1. Write the letter names of the notes of the G MAJOR SCALE on the keyboard below. Use the tetrachord patterns, and be sure each whole step and half step is correct!

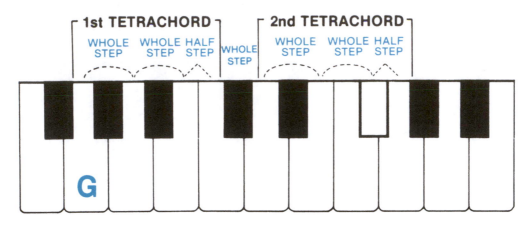

1st TETRACHORD
WHOLE STEP   WHOLE STEP   HALF STEP
WHOLE STEP
2nd TETRACHORD
WHOLE STEP   WHOLE STEP   HALF STEP

G

2. Complete the tetrachord beginning on G. Write one note over each finger number.

3. Complete the tetrachord beginning on D. Write one note under each finger number.

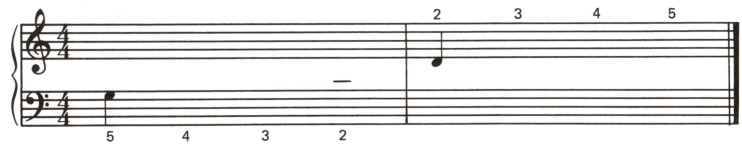

4. Play. Use LH on the 1st tetrachord and RH on the 2nd tetrachord.

Since the G MAJOR SCALE contains ONE SHARP (F♯), music written in the KEY OF G MAJOR has a KEY SIGNATURE of ONE SHARP. The sharps or flats in the key signature are indicated at the beginning of the music, just after the clef sign. They remain in effect throughout the music, or until a new signature appears.

5. Complete a tetrachord beginning on each of the notes below. Write one note under each finger number. The sharp in the key signature will apply to the F♯ in the 2nd tetrachord, so you need not write a sharp before the F.

6. Play with RH. Cross 1 under 3.

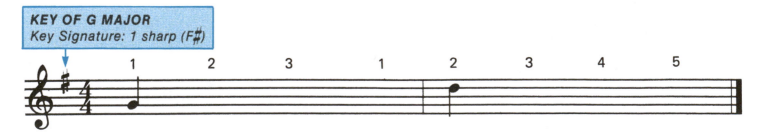

KEY OF G MAJOR
Key Signature: 1 sharp (F♯)

7. Complete a tetrachord beginning on each of the notes below. Write one note over each finger number.

8. Play with LH. Cross 3 over 1.

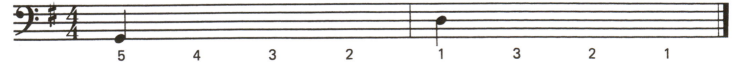

9. Play each of the above 2 scales in REVERSE, starting with the highest note and descending to the lowest. Play the 1st scale with RH, crossing 3 over 1, and the 2nd scale with LH, crossing 1 under 3.

Assign with page 71.

How to Make Any Major Triad

The **1st, 3rd & 5th** notes of any **MAJOR SCALE** make a **MAJOR TRIAD.** It would not be difficult to find any major triad you choose by constructing the major scale of the chosen note, and then playing the 1st, 3rd & 5th notes of the scale.

Here is a **QUICKER** and **EASIER** way to find **ANY** MAJOR TRIAD!

> Choose any note as the **ROOT.**
> Count up **2 whole steps** for the **3rd.**
> Count up **1½ steps** more for the **5th.**

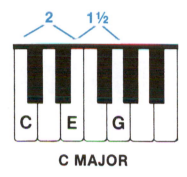

C MAJOR

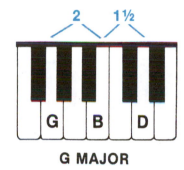

G MAJOR

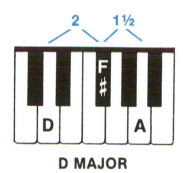

D MAJOR

1. Play each of the above 3 triads in several places on the keyboard, using RH 1 3 5. Carefully observe that there are 2 whole steps between the ROOT and the 3rd, and 1½ steps between the 3rd and the 5th. Repeat, using LH 5 3 1.

2. Build major triads on each of the following keyboard diagrams, using the given note as the ROOT of the triad. Write the letter names of the 3rd & 5th on the keyboards. Remember to skip one letter of the musical alphabet between each note when naming the keys. In other words, **USE THE TRIAD VOCABULARY!**

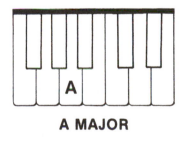

A MAJOR

E MAJOR

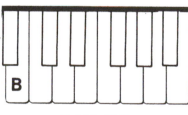

B MAJOR

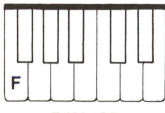

F MAJOR

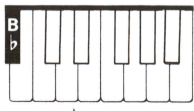

B♭ MAJOR

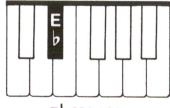

E♭ MAJOR

3. Play each of the above triads in several areas of the keyboard, 1st with RH 1 3 5, then with LH 5 3 1. Say the name of each triad as you play.

How to Play I-IV Progressions Beginning on Any Major Triad

Assign with page 72.

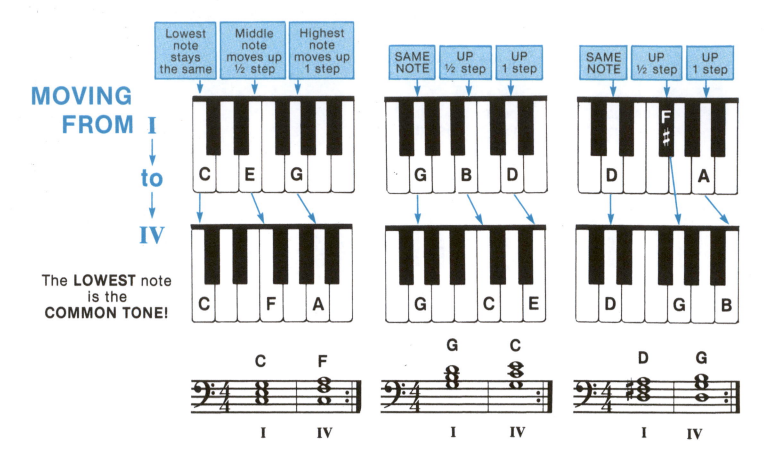

MOVING FROM I to IV

The **LOWEST** note is the **COMMON TONE!**

1. Play the above **I-IV** progressions with LH. Use 5 3 1 on the **I** chords and 5 2 1 on the **IV** chords. Repeat with RH one octave higher, using 1 3 5 on the **I** chords and 1 3 5 on the **IV** chords. Be sure to observe the repeat signs. It is equally important to know how to move from the **IV** chord back to the **I** chord!

2. Complete the following **I-IV** progressions by writing the **IV** chord in the 2nd measure. In each case, the bottom note will be the same in both chords. The middle note will move UP one half-step. The top note will move UP one whole-step.

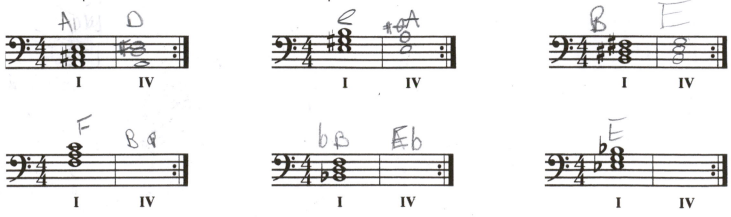

3. Write the chord symbol above each chord. In this progression, the ROOT of the **I** chord is the BOTTOM note. The ROOT of the **IV** chord is the MIDDLE note (the note above the interval of a 4th). All chords are MAJOR TRIADS.

4. Play all of the above **I-IV** progressions, first with LH 5 3 1 - 5 2 1, then with RH one octave higher, using 1 3 5 - 1 3 5. Observe the repeat signs.

How to Play I–V⁷ Progressions Beginning on Any Major Triad

Assign with page 73.

Sarah Motowski

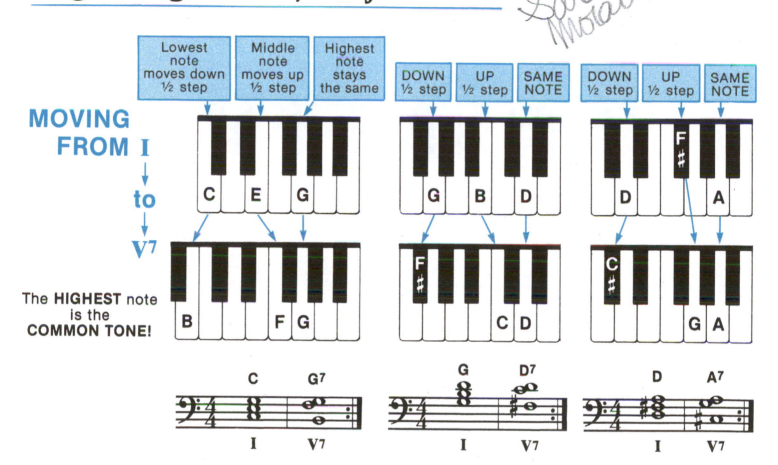

MOVING FROM I to V⁷

The **HIGHEST** note is the **COMMON TONE!**

1. Play the above **I – V⁷** progressions with LH. Use 5 3 1 on the **I** chords, and 5 2 1 on the **V⁷** chords. Repeat with RH one octave higher, using 1 3 5 on the **I** chords and 1 4 5 on the **V⁷** chords. Observe the repeat signs. This gives you practice in the **V⁷ – I** progressions as well!

2. Complete the following **I – V⁷** progressions by writing the **V⁷** chord in the 2nd measure. In each case, the top note will be the same in both chords. The bottom note will move DOWN one half-step, and the middle note will move UP one half-step.

3. Write the chord symbol above each chord. In this progression, the ROOT of the **I** chord is the BOTTOM note. The ROOT of the **V⁷** chord is the TOP note (the note above the interval of a 2nd).

4. Play all of the above **I – V⁷** progressions, first with LH 5 3 1 – 5 2 1, then one octave higher with RH 1 3 5 – 1 4 5. Repeat.

5. Play the following progression in the KEYS OF C & G MAJOR: **I – IV – I – V⁷ – I.**

The Key of F Major

Assign with pages 74–75.

1. Write the letter names of the notes of the F MAJOR SCALE, from *left* to *right* on the keyboard below. Be sure the whole & half steps are correct.

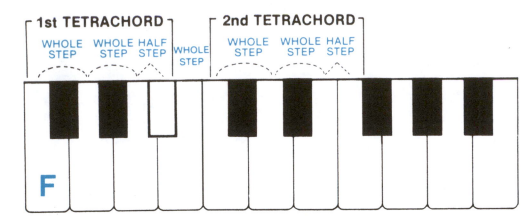

2. Check to be sure you wrote B♭ as the 4th note of the scale. It cannot be called A♯, because scale notes are always in alphabetical order. (You cannot have a scale with two A's and no B's!)

3. Complete the tetrachord beginning on F. Write one note over each finger number.

4. Complete the tetrachord beginning on C. Write one note under each finger number.

5. Play. Use LH on the 1st tetrachord and RH on the 2nd tetrachord.

Since the F MAJOR SCALE contains ONE FLAT (B♭), music written in the KEY OF F MAJOR has a KEY SIGNATURE of ONE FLAT.

6. Complete a tetrachord beginning on each of the following notes below. Write one note over each finger number. The flat in the key signature will apply to the B♭ in the 1st tetrachord, so you need not write the flat before the B.

7. Play with LH. Cross 3 over 1.

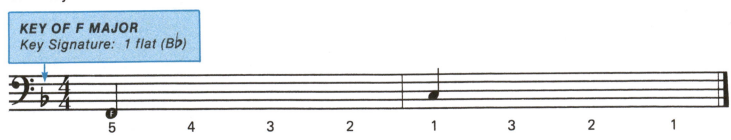

8. Complete a tetrachord beginning on each of the notes below. Write one note under each finger number.

9. Play with RH. Cross 1 under 4.

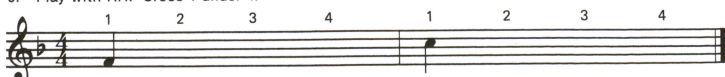

10. Play each of the above 2 scales in REVERSE, starting with the highest note and descending to the lowest. Play the 1st scale with LH, crossing 1 under 3, and the 2nd scale with RH, crossing 4 over 1.

The Primary Chords in F Major

Assign with pages 76–79.

REMEMBER: The 3 PRIMARY CHORDS are derived by building a MAJOR TRIAD on the 1st, 4th and
5th tones of the scale, and adding the interval of a 7th to the one built on the 5th tone.

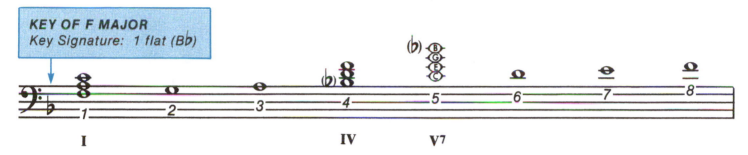

KEY OF F MAJOR
Key Signature: 1 flat (B♭)

I   IV   V7

In the progressions you are studying, the **I** chord remains in ROOT position (with its root on the bottom,
as shown above). The TOP note of the **IV** chord is moved down one octave. The 5th is omitted from the
V7 chord, and the 3rd and 7th are both moved down one octave. The chords now contain COMMON
TONES for smoother progressions, and are easier to play:

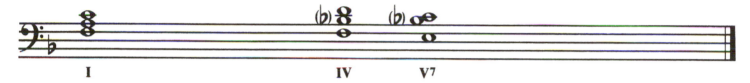

I   IV   V7

1.   Using the method outlined on page 54 of this Theory Book, complete the following **I – IV**
progressions in the KEY OF F MAJOR. Notice how the KEY SIGNATURE takes care of the B flat
that results when you move the 3rd of the **I** chord up one half-step!

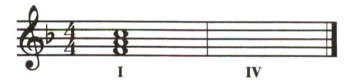

I   IV

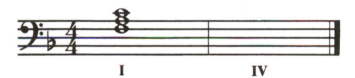

I   IV

2.   Using the method outlined on page 55 of this Theory Book, complete the following **I – V7**
progression in the KEY OF F MAJOR. Once again, the KEY SIGNATURE takes care of the B flat that
results when you move the 3rd of the **I** chord up one half-step.

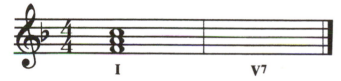

I   V7

I   V7

3.   Write the ROMAN NUMERALS **I, IV, V7** in the boxes below.

4.   Play.

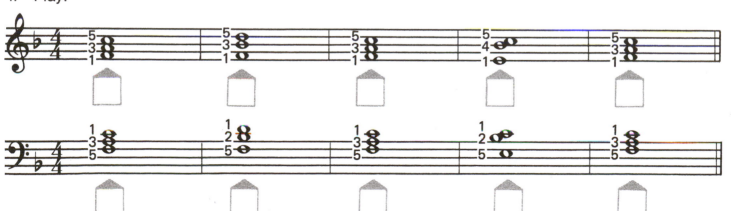

Assign with pages 80–81.

The Key of A Minor (Relative of C Major)

Every MAJOR KEY has a RELATIVE MINOR KEY that has the same KEY SIGNATURE.
The RELATIVE MINOR begins on the 6th TONE of the MAJOR SCALE.

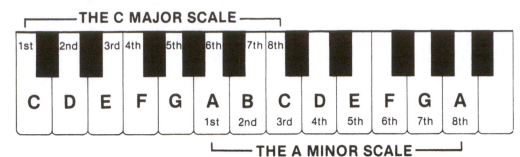

A MINOR is the relative of **C MAJOR**.   Both keys have the same key signature (no sharps, no flats).

THERE ARE 3 KINDS OF MINOR SCALES: the NATURAL, the HARMONIC, & the MELODIC.

THE NATURAL MINOR SCALE. This scale uses *only* the tones of the relative major scale.

KEY OF A MINOR
Key Signature: no #'s, no b's

1.   Play with hands separate.

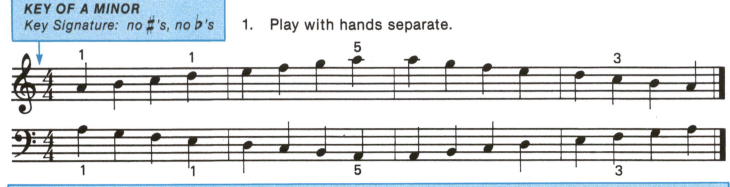

ACCIDENTALS: Any SHARP or FLAT not contained in the key signature is called an ACCIDENTAL.

THE HARMONIC MINOR SCALE.   The 7th tone (G) is raised one half-step,
ASCENDING & DESCENDING.

2.   Add accidental sharps needed to change these NATURAL MINOR scales into HARMONIC
MINOR scales.   3.   Play with hands separate.

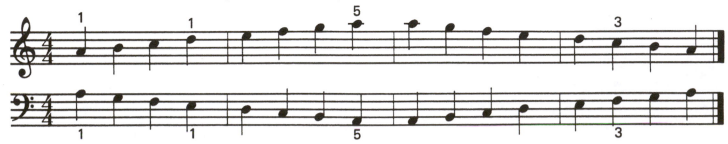

THE MELODIC MINOR SCALE.   In the ASCENDING SCALE, the 6th (F) & 7th (G) are raised one half-step.
The DESCENDING scale is the same as the NATURAL MINOR.

4.   Add accidental sharps needed to change these NATURAL MINOR scales into MELODIC
MINOR scales.   5.   Play with hands separate.

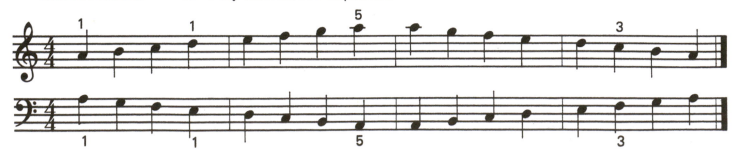

6.   (OPTIONAL) Play all of the above scales with hands together in contrary motion.

More About "Overlapping Pedal"

Assign with pages 82–83.

The following sign is used to indicate **OVERLAPPING PEDAL.**

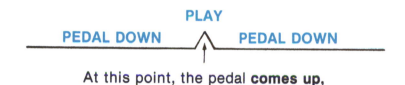

PLAY

PEDAL DOWN ∧ **PEDAL DOWN**

At this point, the pedal **comes up,**
and it goes down again immediately!

The following exercise will make OVERLAPPING PEDAL technique easy!

- Begin with the PEDAL DOWN.
- As you play each note, let the pedal up and press it down again immediately.

  The pedal must come up exactly at the instant the note comes down, as if the pedal "comes up to meet the hand!"

1. Follow the above instructions as you *slowly* play this A HARMONIC MINOR SCALE with the RH.

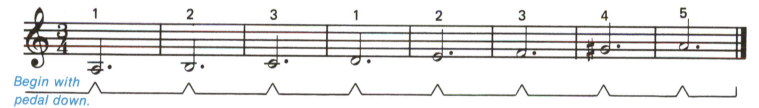

2. Now play the A HARMONIC MINOR SCALE with the LH, pedaling as shown.

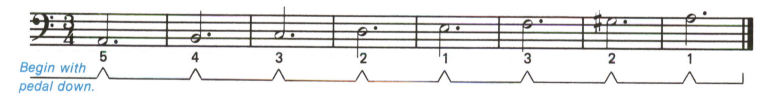

3. Play the following series of RH chords with OVERLAPPING PEDAL.
    Pedal immediately after you play the first chord.

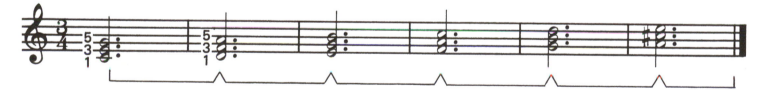

4. Add similar OVERLAPPING PEDAL INDICATIONS below the following LH chords.
    Use a straight edge to draw neat lines.

5. Play and pedal.

Major 3rds & Minor 3rds

Assign with page 84.

3rds that contain 2 whole steps (4 half steps) are called **MAJOR 3rds.**

C & E make a
MAJOR 3rd:
2 WHOLE STEPS
(4 half steps)

3rds that contain only 1½ steps (3 half steps) are called **MINOR 3rds.**

D & F make a
MINOR 3rd:
1½ STEPS
(3 half steps)

1. Under each MAJOR 3rd write a LARGE M. Under each MINOR 3rd write a SMALL m.

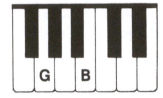

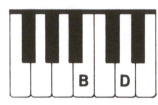

_____3rd   _____3rd   _____3rd   _____3rd

Major Triads & Minor Triads

MAJOR TRIADS consist of a
ROOT, MAJOR 3rd, & PERFECT 5th.

A PERFECT 5TH
contains 7 half steps!

MINOR TRIADS consist of a
ROOT, MINOR 3rd, & PERFECT 5th.

MAJOR TRIAD =

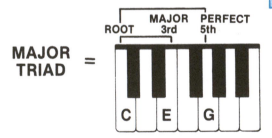

MINOR TRIAD =

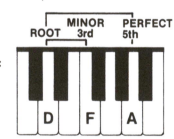

A **QUICK** and **EASY** way to find **ANY** Minor TRIAD:

Choose any note as the **ROOT.**
Count up 1½ **steps** for the **3rd.**
Count up 2 **whole steps** more for the **5th.**

C MINOR (Cm)   Small m = **minor!**

2. Build a MINOR TRIAD on each of the following keyboard diagrams, using the given note as the ROOT. Write the letter names of the 3rd & 5th on the keyboards.
3. Play each triad in several places on the keyboard, 1st with RH 1 3 5, then with LH 5 3 1.

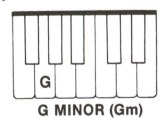

G MINOR (Gm)

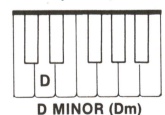

D MINOR (Dm)

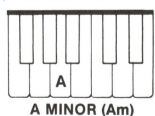

A MINOR (Am)

Any MAJOR TRIAD may be changed to a MINOR TRIAD by lowering the 3rd one half step!

4. Some of the triads below are MAJOR, and some are MINOR. Change those that are major to minor triads by writing a flat sign before the middle note of the triad.

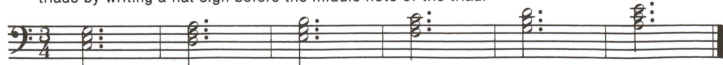

The Primary Chords in A Minor

Assign with pages 84–85.

In minor keys, the PRIMARY CHORDS are built on the 1st, 4th & 5th tones of the HARMONIC MINOR SCALE. The 7th note (G) is made SHARP by an ACCIDENTAL.

Small lower case Roman numerals are used to indicate minor triads (**i** & **iv**).

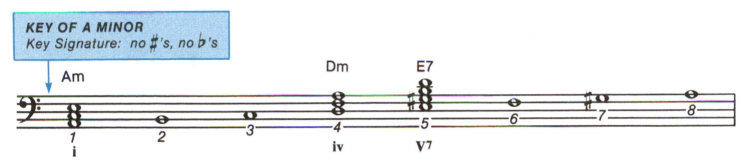

For smooth progressions that contain COMMON TONES, we will be using the **i** chord in ROOT POSITION, while the **iv** & **V7** are moved down. The 5th is omitted from the **V7** chord, as usual.

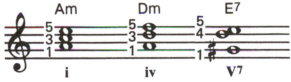

These chords are often played an octave higher:

1. Write the CHORD SYMBOL in the box over each chord.
2. Write the ROMAN NUMERAL in the box below each chord.
3. Play without pedal.
4. Play with pedal.

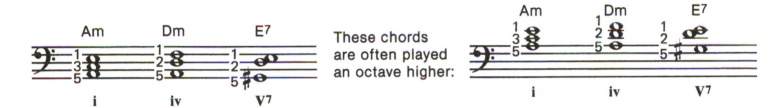

THE PRIMARY CHORDS IN A MINOR FOR RH:

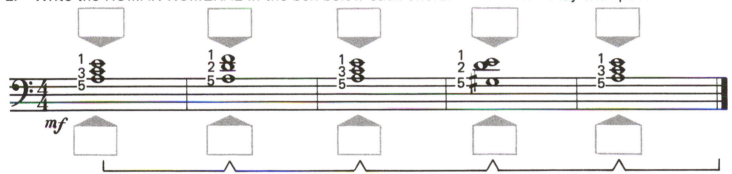

5. Write the CHORD SYMBOL in the box over each chord.
6. Write the ROMAN NUMERAL in the box below each chord.
7. Play without pedal.
8. Play with pedal.

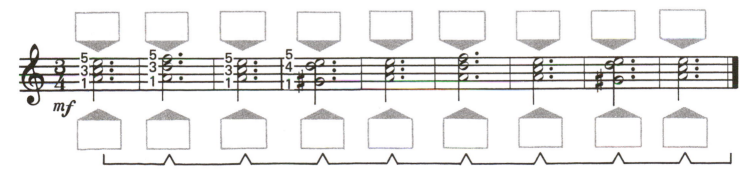

Assign with page 86.

The Key of D Minor (Relative of F Major)

D MINOR is the relative of **F MAJOR**.
Both keys have the same key signature (1 flat, B♭).
REMEMBER: The RELATIVE MINOR begins on the 6th tone of the MAJOR SCALE.

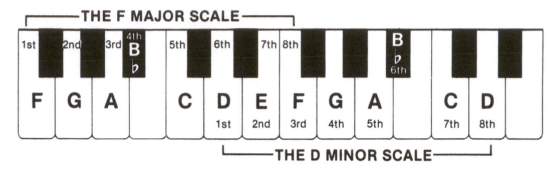

THE NATURAL MINOR SCALE. Uses the same tones as the relative major scale.

1.   Play with hands separate.

KEY OF D MINOR
Key Signature: 1 flat (B♭)

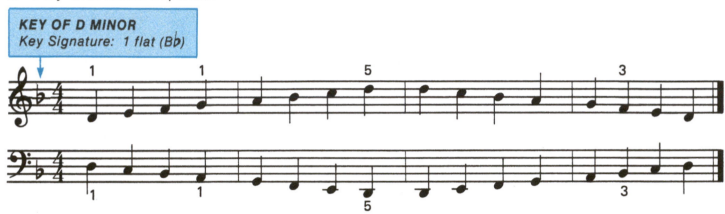

THE HARMONIC MINOR SCALE. The 7th tone (C) is raised one half step, ASCENDING & DESCENDING.

2.   Add accidentals needed to change these NATURAL MINOR scales into HARMONIC MINOR scales.
3.   Play with hands separate.

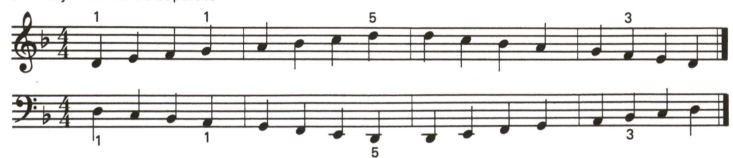

THE MELODIC MINOR SCALE. 6th (B♭) and 7th (C) raised one half step ASCENDING;
descends like natural minor.

4.   Add accidentals needed to change these NATURAL MINOR scales into MELODIC MINOR scales.
5.   Play with hands separate.

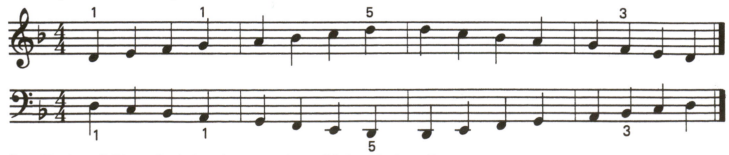

6.   (Optional) Play all of the above scales with hands together.

The Primary Chords in D Minor

Assign with page 88.

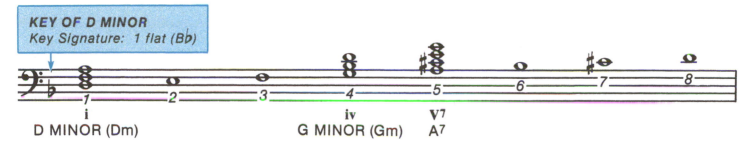

KEY OF D MINOR
Key Signature: 1 flat (B♭)

i · 2 · 3 · iv · V7 · 6 · 7 · 8

D MINOR (Dm)   G MINOR (Gm)   A7

These positions are used for smooth progressions:

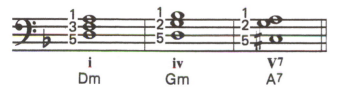   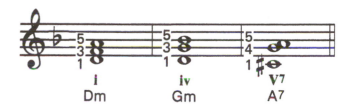

i · iv · V7
Dm · Gm · A7

i · iv · V7
Dm · Gm · A7

1. Play the above progressions several times.

How to Play i–iv & i–V⁷ Progressions Beginning on Any Minor Triad

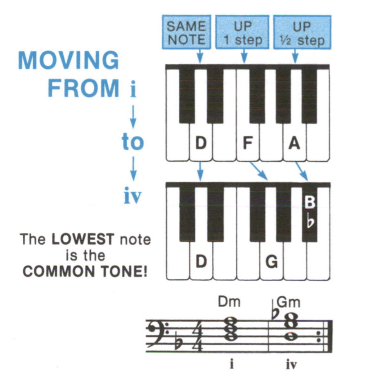

MOVING FROM i to **iv**

| SAME NOTE | UP 1 step | UP ½ step |

The **LOWEST** note is the **COMMON TONE!**

Dm   ♭Gm
i   iv

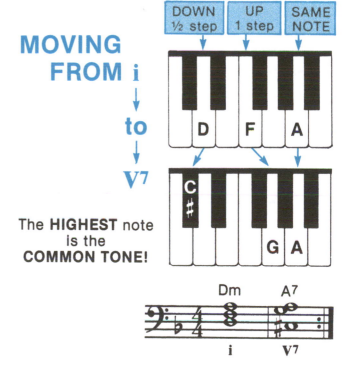

MOVING FROM i to **V7**

| DOWN ½ step | UP 1 step | SAME NOTE |

The **HIGHEST** note is the **COMMON TONE!**

Dm   A7
i   V7

2. Play the above **i – iv** progression, 1st with LH, using 5 3 1 – 5 2 1. Repeat with RH one octave higher, using 1 3 5 – 1 3 5. Repeat.

3. Play the above **i – V7** progression, 1st with LH, using 5 3 1 – 5 2 1. Repeat with RH one octave higher, using 1 3 5 – 1 4 5. Repeat.

4. Complete the following progressions, using the method shown above.
5. Play several times.

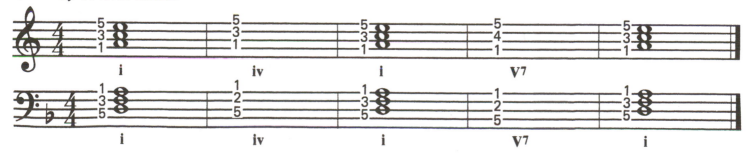

i   iv   i   V7

i   iv   i   V7   i

Eighth Note Triplets

Assign with pages 94–95.

The 3 notes of a TRIPLET are joined with a BEAM.   A *3* is written over or under the center note of each group.

The THREE NOTES of an
EIGHTH NOTE TRIPLET GROUP = ONE QUARTER NOTE.

When a piece contains triplets, count "TRIP-A-LET"
or "ONE & THEN" or any way suggested by your teacher.

1.   Play slowly, counting aloud.

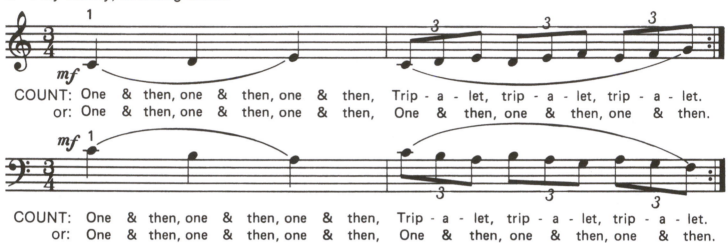

COUNT: One   &   then, one   &   then, one   &   then,   Trip - a - let, trip - a - let, trip - a - let.
  or: One   &   then, one   &   then, one   &   then,   One   &   then, one   &   then, one   &   then.

COUNT: One   &   then, one   &   then, one   &   then,   Trip - a - let, trip - a - let, trip - a - let.
  or: One   &   then, one   &   then, one   &   then,   One   &   then, one   &   then, one   &   then.

Review Puzzle

2.   Draw lines connecting the dots on the matching boxes.

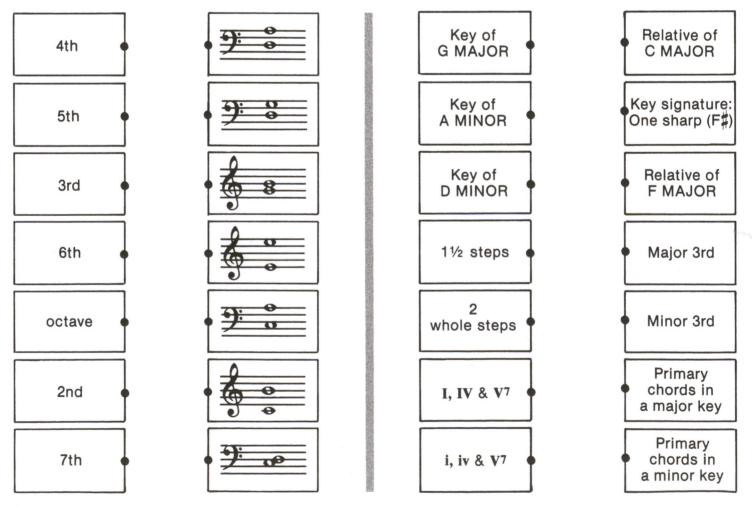

Score 4 for each box correctly matched.   Perfect score = 112.   **YOUR SCORE** _____.